CGP

GCSE OCR Gateway
Core Science
Foundation — the Basics
The Revision Guide

This book is for anyone doing **GCSE OCR Gateway Core Science**
at Foundation Level, with a predicted grade of D or below.
(If you're not sure what your predicted grade is, your teacher will be able to tell you.)

All the important topics are explained in a clear, straightforward
way to help you get all the marks you can in the exam.

And of course, there are some daft bits to make the whole
thing vaguely entertaining for you.

What CGP is all about

Our sole aim here at CGP is to produce the highest
quality books — carefully written, immaculately presented
and dangerously close to being funny.

Then we work our socks off to get them out to you — at the cheapest possible prices.

Contents

MODULE B2 — UNDERSTANDING OUR ENVIRONMENT

MODULE C2 — CHEMICAL RESOURCES

MODULE P2 — LIVING FOR THE FUTURE

Published by CGP

Editors:
Katie Braid, Katherine Craig, Emma Elder, Ben Fletcher, Edmund Robinson, Helen Ronan,
Hayley Thompson, Dawn Wright.

ISBN: 978 1 84762 716 2

With thanks to Rosie McCurrie and Karen Wells for the proofreading.

With thanks to Jeremy Cooper, Janet Cruse-Sawyer and Ian Francis for the reviewing.

With thanks to Jan Greenway, Laura Jakubowski and Laura Stoney for the copyright research.

With thanks to iStockphoto.com for permission to use the image on page 21.

With thanks to Science Photo Library for permission to use the image on page 50.

GORE-TEX®, GORE®, and designs are registered trademarks of W L Gore & Associates.
This book contains copyrighted material reproduced with the permission of
W.L. Gore and Associates. Copyright 2011 W.L. Gore & Associates.

Groovy website: www.cgpbooks.co.uk

Printed by Elanders Ltd, Newcastle upon Tyne.
Jolly bits of clipart from CorelDRAW®

Based on the classic CGP style created by Richard Parsons.

The Scientific Process

For your <u>exams</u> and your <u>controlled assessment</u>, you need to know how the world of science <u>works</u>.

A Hypothesis is an Explanation of Something

1) Scientists <u>OBSERVE</u> (look at) things they <u>don't understand</u>.
2) They then come up with an <u>explanation</u> for what they've seen.
3) This explanation is called a <u>HYPOTHESIS</u>.

For Example:

A scientist is looking at <u>why</u> people have <u>spots</u>.

He notices that everyone with spots <u>picks their nose</u>.

The scientist thinks that the spots might be <u>caused</u> by people picking their nose.

So the <u>hypothesis</u> is: **"Spots are caused by picking your nose."**

---

4) Next, scientists need to <u>check</u> whether the <u>hypothesis</u> is <u>RIGHT or NOT</u>.
5) They do this by making a <u>PREDICTION</u> and <u>TESTING</u> it.

For Example:

A prediction is something like: **"People who pick their nose will have spots."**

Sometimes a hypothesis and a prediction are the same thing.

---

6) If tests show that the <u>prediction</u> is <u>RIGHT</u>, then there's <u>EVIDENCE</u> (signs) that the <u>hypothesis is right</u> too.
7) If tests show that the <u>prediction</u> is <u>WRONG</u>, then the <u>hypothesis</u> is probably <u>wrong</u> as well.

Other Scientists Test the Hypothesis by Making Predictions

1) It's <u>NOT enough</u> for <u>one scientist</u> to do tests to see if the hypothesis is right or not.
2) <u>Other scientists</u> test the hypothesis as well.
3) Sometimes these scientists will find <u>more evidence</u> that the <u>hypothesis is RIGHT</u>.
4) When this happens the hypothesis is <u>accepted</u> and goes into <u>books</u> for people to learn.

When scientists check each other's work, it's called peer review.

5) Sometimes the scientists will find <u>evidence</u> that shows the <u>hypothesis is WRONG</u>.
6) Or sometimes <u>new evidence</u> will come up that the hypothesis <u>can't explain</u>.
7) When this happens the scientists have to start <u>all over again</u>. Sad times.

Investigations

Scientists carry out <u>investigations</u>. You'll have to do some too — so here's what they're all about.

Investigations Have to be Fair Tests

1) You need to make sure your investigation is a <u>FAIR TEST</u>. You must...

ONLY CHANGE ONE THING. EVERYTHING ELSE must be kept the SAME.

2) The thing that you <u>CHANGE</u> is called the <u>INDEPENDENT</u> variable.
3) The things that you <u>keep the SAME</u> are called <u>CONTROL</u> variables.
4) The thing that's <u>MEASURED</u> is called the <u>DEPENDENT</u> variable.

Example: Investigation to see how changing the <u>amount of light</u> changes <u>how tall a plant grows</u>

<u>Change</u> the amount of <u>light</u> the plant gets (the <u>independent variable</u>).

Keep <u>everything else</u> the <u>same</u> (the <u>control variables</u>).

Anybody out there...?

Different amounts of light

Same temperature

Same type of plant

Same amount of water

The <u>dependent variable</u> is <u>how tall the plant grows</u> — that's what you're <u>measuring</u>.

The Equipment has to be Right for the Job

1) You need to choose the <u>right equipment</u> for your investigation.
2) For example, choose <u>measuring equipment</u> that will let you measure stuff really closely.

If you need to measure out <u>11 ml</u>, this measuring cylinder would be great. It's the <u>right size</u> and you can <u>see</u> where 11 ml is.

This measuring cylinder isn't as good. It's <u>too big</u> and you <u>can't really see</u> where 11 ml is.

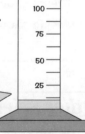

Investigations Can be Dangerous

1) A <u>HAZARD</u> is something that <u>could cause HARM</u>.
2) Hazards are things like... <u>microorganisms</u> (e.g. bacteria) <u>chemicals</u> <u>fire</u> <u>electricity</u>

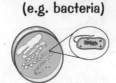

3) Scientists need to <u>REDUCE the RISK</u> of hazards causing harm. For example:

- If you're using a <u>Bunsen burner</u>, stand it on a <u>heat-proof mat</u>.
- This will <u>reduce the risk</u> of <u>starting a fire</u>.

Collecting Data

When you're collecting your data, you need to think about <u>repeating</u> your investigation.

The More Times You Repeat the Investigation the Better

1) When you're doing an investigation you need to <u>REPEAT it</u> — <u>three times</u> is usually enough.

2) Then you can work out the <u>mean</u> (average) of the data — see below.

3) <u>Repeating</u> your investigation makes your results more <u>RELIABLE</u>.

For Example: You want to know how long a reaction takes at 10 °C, 20 °C and 30 °C

Do the reaction <u>THREE TIMES</u> at <u>EACH temperature</u>. Time <u>how long</u> it takes <u>each time</u>.

Reaction time at <u>10 °C</u>

Reaction time at <u>20 °C</u>

Reaction time at <u>30 °C</u>

You can then put all the results into a <u>table</u> and work out the <u>mean reaction time</u> (see below).

Data Needs to be Organised

<u>TABLES</u> are dead useful for <u>organising data</u>.

Temperature (°C)	Repeat 1 (s)	Repeat 2 (s)	Repeat 3 (s)
10	31	30	29
20	22	19	20
30	10	11	11

Make sure that each column has a heading

Don't forget the units

You Might Have to Work Out the Mean

1) If you've <u>repeated</u> an investigation you need to work out the <u>MEAN</u> (average).

2) Just <u>ADD TOGETHER</u> the results. Then <u>DIVIDE</u> by the total number of results.

Temperature (°C)	Repeat 1 (s)	Repeat 2 (s)	Repeat 3 (s)	Mean (s)
10	31	30	29	$\dfrac{(31 + 30 + 29) = 30}{3}$
20	22	19	20	$\dfrac{(22 + 19 + 20) = 20.3}{3}$
30	10	11	11	$\dfrac{(10 + 11 + 11) = 10.7}{3}$

Add together the results

Divide by 3 (because there are three results for 10 °C)

Presenting Data

Scientists just <u>love</u> presenting data as <u>graphs</u> (weirdos)...

Bar Charts <u>are</u> Used When You've Got Categories

1) <u>CATEGORIES</u> are things like blood type or ice cream flavour. You <u>can't</u> get results <u>in-between categories</u>.

2) If you're measuring something that comes in <u>categories</u> you should use a <u>BAR</u> chart to show the data.

3) There are some <u>rules</u> you need to follow for <u>drawing</u> bar charts...

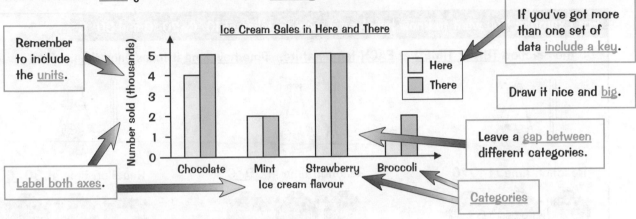

Remember to include the <u>units</u>.

If you've got more than one set of data <u>include a key</u>.

Draw it nice and <u>big</u>.

Leave a <u>gap between</u> different categories.

<u>Label both axes</u>.

<u>Categories</u>

You Need to be Able to Draw <u>Line</u> Graphs

1) If you're measuring something that can have <u>ANY value</u> you should use a <u>LINE</u> graph to show the data.

2) For example, <u>temperatures</u> and people's <u>heights</u> would be shown using a line graph.

3) Here are the <u>rules</u> for drawing line graphs...

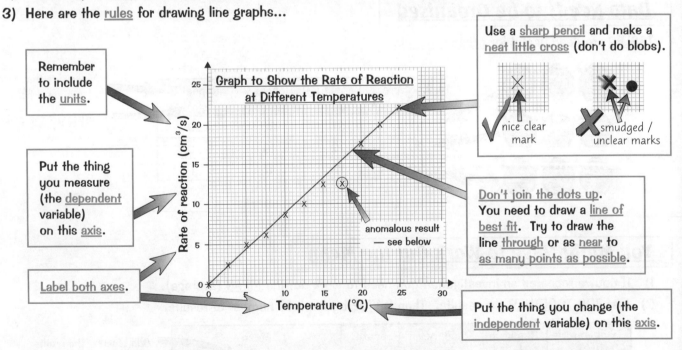

Remember to include the <u>units</u>.

Put the thing you measure (the <u>dependent</u> variable) on this <u>axis</u>.

Label both axes.

Use a <u>sharp pencil</u> and make a <u>neat little cross</u> (don't do blobs).

nice clear mark

smudged / unclear marks

<u>Don't join the dots up</u>. You need to draw a <u>line of best fit</u>. Try to draw the line <u>through</u> or as <u>near</u> to as <u>many points as possible</u>.

Put the thing you change (the <u>independent</u> variable) on this <u>axis</u>.

You Can Get <u>Anomalous Results</u>

1) Sometimes you get a result that <u>doesn't seem to FIT IN</u> with the rest at all.

2) These results are called <u>ANOMALOUS RESULTS</u>.

3) You can <u>IGNORE</u> them when you're working out <u>means</u>.

4) But you should try to find out what <u>caused them</u>.

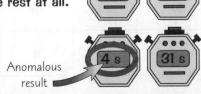

Anomalous result

Drawing Conclusions

So, you've organised and presented your data. Next thing to do is to write a <u>conclusion</u>.

You Can Only Conclude What the Data Shows and NO MORE

To come to a conclusion, <u>look at your data</u> and <u>say what pattern you see</u>.

<u>EXAMPLE</u>: <u>Pea plants</u> were grown with <u>different fertilisers</u>. The table below shows how <u>tall</u> the plants grew.

Fertiliser	Mean growth / mm
A	13.5
B	19.5
C	5.5

<u>CONCLUSION</u>: Fertiliser <u>B</u> makes <u>pea plants</u> grow taller than fertiliser A or fertiliser C.

Be careful with conclusions — make sure you <u>DON'T</u> say <u>MORE</u> than what the results show. For example...
*   You <u>can't</u> say that fertiliser B makes <u>any plant</u> grow taller than fertiliser A or C — just <u>pea plants</u>.
*   You <u>can't</u> say that fertiliser B is the <u>best</u> fertiliser to use on pea plants — there could be <u>another fertiliser</u> out there that's <u>even better</u>. All you can say is it's <u>better than fertiliser A or C</u>.

Line Graphs Show Patterns in Data

1) Line graphs are great for <u>showing the relationship</u> (the link) between two things.
2) The relationship is called a <u>CORRELATION</u>. You need to know about <u>three types of correlation</u>...

<u>POSITIVE CORRELATION</u>

As one thing <u>increases</u> so does the other.

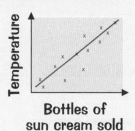

As the <u>temperature increases</u> the amount of <u>sun cream</u> sold also <u>increases</u>.

<u>NEGATIVE CORRELATION</u>

As one thing <u>increases</u> the other <u>decreases</u>.

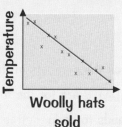

As the <u>temperature increases</u> the number of <u>hats</u> sold <u>decreases</u>.

<u>NO CORRELATION</u>

There's <u>no relationship</u> between the two things.

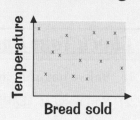

The temperature has <u>no effect</u> on the amount of bread sold.

3) Even if there <u>IS</u> a <u>correlation</u>, it <u>DOESN'T</u> always mean that a change in one thing is <u>CAUSING</u> the change in the other. For example...

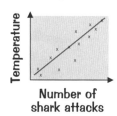

*   There's a <u>POSITIVE CORRELATION</u> between the <u>temperature of the sea</u> and the <u>number of shark attacks</u> (when the water is <u>warmer</u> there are <u>more attacks</u>).
*   This <u>DOESN'T</u> mean that sharks are more likely to attack in warm water — it's just that there are <u>more people in the water</u> to attack when it's warm.

How Science Works

Using Equations

Sometimes in science you have to do some <u>maths</u>. Boo. Hiss.
But if you learn how to <u>use equations</u>, they're a great way to pick up <u>marks</u> in the exam.

Most of the Equations You Need Are Written in the Exam Paper

1) Equations can <u>LOOK tricky</u>.

2) But for <u>all</u> equations, all you have to do is
<u>TIMES</u> OR <u>DIVIDE ONE NUMBER BY ANOTHER</u>.

3) It's really useful to <u>know</u> equations <u>off by heart</u>.

4) But <u>MOST</u> of the equations you need will be on
an <u>EQUATION SHEET</u> in the exam paper. Hooray.

5) You just have to know <u>WHICH EQUATION to use</u> and <u>HOW to use it</u>.

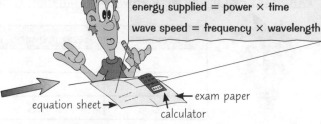

energy supplied = power × time

wave speed = frequency × wavelength

equation sheet → | ← exam paper
calculator

<u>Example:</u> A wave has a <u>frequency</u> of 20 Hz and a <u>wavelength</u> of 5 m. What is its <u>speed</u>?

1 Decide <u>WHICH EQUATION</u> to use and <u>WRITE IT OUT</u>. → If you can't remember the equation, look for one on the equation sheet with <u>frequency</u>, <u>wavelength</u> and <u>speed</u> in it. → wave speed = frequency × wavelength

2 <u>PLUG IN THE NUMBERS</u>.
Sometimes you'll need to get them in the right units first — see below. → Frequency is 20 Hz, and wavelength is 5 m.
Write these numbers under the equation. → wave speed = frequency × wavelength
wave speed = 20 Hz × 5 m

3 <u>WORK OUT</u> the answer with a <u>calculator</u>. → wave speed = 20 Hz × 5 m
= 100

4 Don't forget the <u>UNITS</u>. → The <u>units</u> of <u>speed</u> are <u>m/s</u>. → wave speed = <u>100 m/s</u>

Check Your Units

1) Before you plug the numbers in, check the <u>numbers</u> in the question have the <u>RIGHT UNITS</u>.

2) You need to <u>LEARN</u> what the <u>RIGHT UNITS</u> are for the things in the equations.

3) For example, <u>wavelength</u> <u>ALWAYS</u> needs to be in <u>metres</u> (m) to use the wave speed equation.

4) If you're given a wavelength in <u>centimetres</u>, you have to <u>change it to metres BEFORE you use the equation</u>.

<u>Another Example:</u> Find the <u>energy supplied</u>, in kWh, by a <u>1.5 kW</u> hair drier in <u>30 minutes</u>.

- Work out <u>which equation</u> you need to use: → energy supplied = power × time
- The <u>power</u> is <u>1.5 kW</u>. The <u>time</u> is <u>30 minutes</u>.
- But to get energy in <u>kWh</u> (kilowatt-hours), the <u>time</u> needs to be in <u>HOURS</u>.
- There are <u>60 minutes in an hour</u>. So 30 minutes = 30 ÷ 60 = <u>0.5 hours</u>.
- Now you can <u>plug the numbers</u> into the equation: energy supplied = power × time
energy supplied = 1.5 kW × 0.5 h
energy suppled = <u>0.75 kWh</u>

5) Remember you <u>always</u> need to give the <u>right units</u> with your <u>ANSWER</u> too.

Fitness and Blood Pressure

Ahh. Fitness and blood pressure. Just the stuff to get your <u>blood pumping</u> and your brain in gear.

Being Fit <u>is</u> Not <u>the Same as Being Healthy</u>

Being <u>HEALTHY</u> means you <u>don't have</u> a <u>disease</u>.

Being <u>FIT</u> means you find <u>physical activity</u> (like exercise) <u>easy</u>.

You can <u>MEASURE</u> someone's <u>FITNESS</u> by measuring their:

STRENGTH

AGILITY

SPEED

FLEXIBILITY

STAMINA

Someone with good <u>agility</u> would be good at things like <u>jumping</u> and <u>climbing</u>.

Someone with good <u>stamina</u> would be able to keep <u>running</u> for a <u>long time</u>.

<u>Blood</u> <u>is</u> <u>Pumped</u> <u>Around Your Body</u>

When your <u>heart</u> <u>CONTRACTS</u> (squeezes), your blood gets <u>pumped</u> around your body.

This <u>INCREASES</u> your blood <u>pressure</u>.

Blood <u>pressure</u> needs to be fairly <u>HIGH</u>. This is so the blood can reach <u>every part</u> of your <u>body</u>.

z z z

blood pressure

1) Blood pressure is <u>HIGHEST</u> when the heart <u>CONTRACTS</u>. This is called the <u>SYSTOLIC PRESSURE</u>.

2) Blood pressure is <u>LOWEST</u> when the heart <u>RELAXES</u>. This is called the <u>DIASTOLIC PRESSURE</u>.

Blood pressure is measured in units called <u>mmHg</u>.

<u>Your Blood Pressure</u> <u>Can Be Too High</u>

Sometimes your blood pressure can get <u>too high</u>. These things can all <u>increase</u> your blood pressure:

<u>SMOKING</u>

being <u>OVERWEIGHT</u>

too much <u>ALCOHOL</u>

<u>STRESS</u>

Blood pressure can be <u>LOWERED</u> by doing regular <u>EXERCISE</u> and eating a <u>BALANCED DIET</u>.

Practice Questions

1) "Being fit is the <u>same</u> as being healthy." True or false?
2) Give <u>two</u> things that can <u>increase</u> your <u>blood pressure</u>.

High Blood Pressure and Heart Disease

Heart disease is pretty nasty — and it can be caused by smoking and eating too much salt and fat.

Smoking Can Lead to Heart Disease

Cigarette smoke has NICOTINE and CARBON MONOXIDE in it. These can cause heart disease.

1) NICOTINE increases your HEART RATE.

2) This increases your BLOOD PRESSURE, which can cause HEART DISEASE.

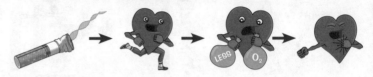

1) CARBON MONOXIDE makes your blood carry LESS OXYGEN.

2) To make up for this your HEART RATE increases.

3) This increases your BLOOD PRESSURE, which can cause HEART DISEASE.

Eating Too Much Saturated Fat Can Lead to Heart Disease

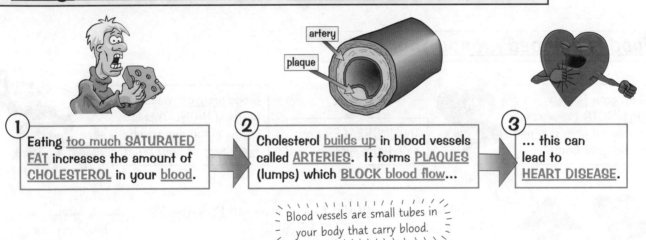

artery

plaque

1) Eating too much SATURATED FAT increases the amount of CHOLESTEROL in your blood.

2) Cholesterol builds up in blood vessels called ARTERIES. It forms PLAQUES (lumps) which BLOCK blood flow...

3) ... this can lead to HEART DISEASE.

Blood vessels are small tubes in your body that carry blood.

Eating Too Much Salt Can Also Lead to Heart Disease

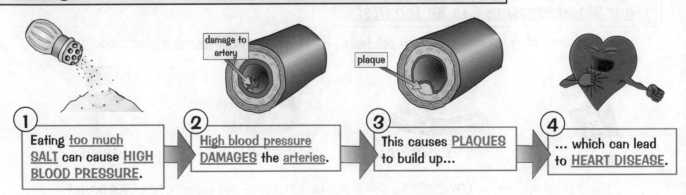

damage to artery

plaque

1) Eating too much SALT can cause HIGH BLOOD PRESSURE.

2) High blood pressure DAMAGES the arteries.

3) This causes PLAQUES to build up...

4) ... which can lead to HEART DISEASE.

Practice Questions

1) Name two things found in cigarette smoke.

2) Name two things you eat that can cause heart disease.

Eating Healthily

You need a balanced diet to give you energy and make sure that everything keeps working properly.

A Balanced Diet Keeps You Healthy

Your DIET is the food you eat. A BALANCED DIET is a diet that's got everything you need to stay healthy. A balanced diet has:

CARBOHYDRATES
Give you energy.

Made up of sugars like glucose.

FATS
Give you energy.

Made up of fatty acids and glycerol.

PROTEINS
Help your muscles grow. Sometimes give you energy.

Made up of amino acids.

FIBRE
Stops constipation (difficulty pooing).

VITAMINS
You need vitamin C to stop you getting an illness called scurvy.

MINERALS
You need iron for healthy red blood cells.

WATER
Stops dehydration (where the body doesn't have enough water).

A Balanced Diet is Different for Different People

Different people need different things in their diet. What they need depends on:

AGE

Children and teenagers need lots of protein because they're still growing.

GENDER

Women lose iron in blood during their period. They need to eat more iron to replace what they lose.

ACTIVITY

Active people need more carbohydrates for energy.

Some People Choose to Eat a Different Diet

Some people choose not to eat some foods for all sorts of reasons:

PERSONAL REASONS
For example, VEGETARIANS don't eat meat. VEGANS don't eat any foods from animals, including eggs and milk.

RELIGIOUS REASONS
For example, Hindus don't eat beef because they believe cows are SACRED.

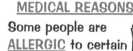

MEDICAL REASONS
Some people are ALLERGIC to certain foods (like nuts). These foods make them ill.

Practice Questions

1) Name three things you need as part of a balanced diet.
2) Why do teenagers need lots of protein?
3) What don't vegans eat?

Diet Problems

Not eating enough food can affect your health. So can eating too much food.

Eating Too Little Can Cause Problems

1) If you don't eat enough PROTEIN you can get an illness called KWASHIORKOR.

2) Lots of people in developing (poor) countries get Kwashiorkor because:

There are LOTS OF PEOPLE but NOT ENOUGH FOOD.

There isn't a lot of MONEY to spend on FARMING.

3) The amount of protein you need to eat each day is called your EAR (Estimated Average daily Requirement). This is how you work out your EAR:

$$\text{EAR (in g)} = 0.6 \times \text{body mass (in kg)}$$

Body mass is just how much you weigh.

4) Some people don't eat enough because they're worried about their weight. They might have no confidence about the way they look.

5) But if you don't eat enough food you can get really ill. For example, you could have a heart attack. You could even die.

Eating Too Much Can Lead to Obesity

1) OBESITY means being very overweight.

2) It's caused by:

 TOO MUCH FOOD  NOT ENOUGH EXERCISE

3) If you're obese you're more likely to get diabetes, arthritis, heart disease and breast cancer.

Body Mass Index Shows If You're Underweight or Overweight

1) The BODY MASS INDEX (BMI) helps decide whether someone is underweight, normal, overweight or obese.

2) It's worked out using their HEIGHT and WEIGHT:

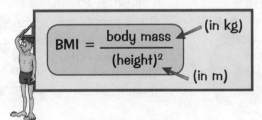

$$\text{BMI} = \frac{\text{body mass} \ (\text{in kg})}{(\text{height})^2 \ (\text{in m})}$$

Body Mass Index	Weight Description
below 18.5	underweight
18.5 - 24.9	normal
25 - 29.9	overweight
over 30	obese

The table shows how BMI is used to describe people's weight.

Practice Questions

1) Give one reason why Kwashiorkor is common in developing countries.

2) Write down one cause of obesity.

Infectious Disease

Your body <u>fights off attacks</u> every day...

Infectious **Diseases are Caused by** Pathogens

1) An <u>INFECTIOUS DISEASE</u> can be <u>passed on</u> to another person. For example, flu.

2) Infectious diseases are caused by <u>MICROORGANISMS</u> called <u>PATHOGENS</u>.

3) There are four main types of pathogen:

Microorganisms are really tiny creatures.

Type of pathogen:	FUNGI	BACTERIA	VIRUSES	PROTOZOA
Examples of illnesses caused:	Athlete's foot	Cholera	Flu	Malaria

4) Pathogens cause the <u>SYMPTOMS</u> of a disease, for example a <u>rash</u>.

5) They cause symptoms by: DAMAGING CELLS   MAKING TOXINS (poisons)

6) A <u>NON-INFECTIOUS DISEASE</u> can't be passed on to another person. For example, diabetes.

7) <u>Genetic disorders</u> are non-infectious diseases. They're caused by <u>genes</u> that <u>don't work properly</u>.

Malaria *is an* Infectious Disease

Malaria is caused by a <u>PROTOZOAN</u>.

The protozoan lives off <u>MOSQUITOES</u>.

Mosquitoes carry the protozoan between <u>animals</u> and <u>people</u>.

Mosquitoes <u>infect people</u> with malaria when they <u>BITE</u> them.

You need to know these fancy scientific words:

1) The malarial protozoan is a <u>PARASITE</u>. Parasites are creatures that <u>live off</u> other creatures.

2) Mosquitoes are <u>VECTORS</u>. This means they <u>carry a disease</u> without getting it themselves.

3) The animals mosquitoes feed on are called <u>HOSTS</u>.

PARASITE   VECTOR   HOST

Diseases *are* More Common *in* Some Places

1) The <u>INCIDENCE OF A DISEASE</u> is <u>how common</u> a disease is.

2) Many diseases are <u>MORE COMMON</u> in:

HOT PLACES

POORER COUNTRIES

Practice Questions

1) "An <u>infectious disease</u> can be passed on to another person." True or false?

2) "Mosquitoes are <u>vectors</u>." What does this mean?

More On Infectious Disease

Diseases <u>suck</u>. That's why your body has got lots of ways of defending itself.

The Body Has Four Main Ways of Keeping Out Pathogens

<u>SKIN</u> keeps pathogens out.

Hydrochloric <u>ACID</u> in the <u>STOMACH</u> kills pathogens.

<u>STICKY MUCUS</u> in the <u>AIRWAYS</u> traps pathogens.

<u>BLOOD CLOTS</u> (scabs) keep pathogens out of cuts.

Your Immune System Destroys Pathogens

1) Your <u>IMMUNE SYSTEM</u> destroys pathogens that get into your body.

2) The most important bit of the immune system is the <u>WHITE BLOOD CELLS</u>. They do <u>two</u> things:

1. Digest Pathogens

White blood cells <u>ENGULF</u> (surround) the pathogens...

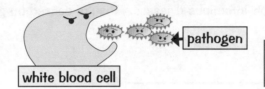

white blood cell

pathogen

... then they <u>DIGEST</u> (eat) them.

2. Make Antibodies

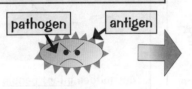

pathogen   antigen

Hello!

white blood cell

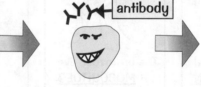

antibody

① Pathogens have bits on their surface called <u>ANTIGENS</u>.

② White blood cells <u>RECOGNISE</u> the <u>antigens</u>.

③ White blood cells then make <u>ANTIBODIES</u>.

④ Antibodies <u>lock on</u> to antigens and <u>KILL</u> the pathogen.

Immunisation Stops You Getting Infections

1) A <u>disease CAN'T make you SICK</u> if you're <u>IMMUNE</u> to it.

2) You can be <u>made</u> immune to some diseases by being <u>IMMUNISED</u> (vaccinated).

3) <u>IMMUNISATION</u> is a type of <u>ACTIVE IMMUNITY</u>.

- <u>Active immunity</u> is where you <u>make your OWN antibodies</u> to fight off diseases.
- <u>PASSIVE IMMUNITY</u> is where you get <u>antibodies</u> from <u>someone else</u>.
  For example, <u>babies</u> get antibodies from their <u>mums</u> when they drink <u>breast milk</u>.

Practice Questions

1) Give <u>two</u> ways that your <u>body keeps</u> out pathogens.

2) What <u>type</u> of <u>blood cell</u> destroys pathogens?

Cancer and Drug Development

Ever wondered how <u>drugs</u> are <u>developed</u>? No, me neither. But it's actually quite <u>interesting</u>.
First up though, a little bit on <u>cancer</u>.

You Can Reduce the Risk of Getting Some Cancers

Your colon is part of your digestive system.

Having a <u>healthy lifestyle</u> and <u>diet</u> can make it less likely you'll get some <u>cancers</u>.
For example:

<u>NOT SMOKING</u> makes it less likely you'll get <u>lung cancer</u>.

Eating <u>MORE FIBRE</u> makes it less likely you'll get <u>colon cancer</u>.

Antibiotics and Antivirals Are Types of Drugs

<u>ANTIBIOTICS KILL BACTERIA</u>...

... but <u>NOT VIRUSES</u>.

<u>ANTIVIRALS STOP VIRUSES</u> from <u>reproducing</u> (copying themselves)...

Nooooo!

... <u>BUT</u> have <u>NO</u> effect on <u>BACTERIA</u>.

Drugs Need to be Tested

<u>New drugs</u> have to be <u>TESTED</u> before they can be used. This is to make sure they're <u>SAFE</u> and that they <u>WORK</u>.

(1) <u>COMPUTER MODELS</u> are used to...
- <u>Find</u> drugs that might be useful.
- <u>Predict</u> how a <u>drug</u> will work on <u>humans</u>.

(2) <u>HUMAN SAMPLES</u> are used to...
- See how <u>HUMAN CELLS</u> respond to the drug.

(3) <u>ANIMALS</u> are used to...
- Test the drug on <u>living creatures</u>.

Some people think it's <u>CRUEL</u> to test on animals. Others think it's the <u>SAFEST</u> way to make sure a drug isn't <u>DANGEROUS</u>.

Practice Questions
1) What do <u>antibiotics</u> kill?
2) Give <u>two</u> reasons for <u>testing drugs</u> before they're used.

Drugs: Use and Harm

Drugs can be legal or illegal. Both might be in the exam — so get reading.

Drugs Can Help You or Harm You

1) Some drugs are USEFUL, for example, antibiotics. But some drugs can HARM you.

2) You can buy some drugs at a chemist. To get other drugs you need a PRESCRIPTION.

A prescription is a note from your doctor.

Must have drugs...

3) Some people get ADDICTED to drugs. Without them they get WITHDRAWAL SYMPTOMS, like being sick.

4) TOLERANCE is where you need more of a drug to get the same effect.

5) REHABILITATION can help people get off drugs.

You Need to Know All About These Drugs...

Drug	Examples	Effects
DEPRESSANTS	alcohol, solvents (glue), tamazepan (sleeping pills)	Slow down the brain.
STIMULANTS	caffeine, ecstasy, nicotine	Make the brain work faster.
PAINKILLERS	paracetamol, aspirin	Stop you feeling pain.
PERFORMANCE ENHANCERS	anabolic steroids	Help build muscle.
HALLUCINOGENS	LSD	Change what you see and hear.

Some Drugs are Illegal

ILLEGAL DRUGS are put into THREE main categories:

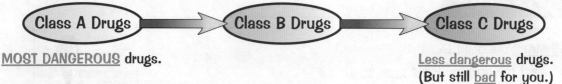

Class A Drugs → Class B Drugs → Class C Drugs

MOST DANGEROUS drugs.

Less dangerous drugs. (But still bad for you.)

1) Using class A drugs could get you a long prison sentence.

2) Using class C drugs could get you a warning or a short prison sentence.

Practice Questions

1) What effect do stimulants have on the body?

2) "Class A drugs are the least dangerous drugs." True or false?

Alcohol

<u>Drinking</u> a lot of alcohol doesn't do you much good. Big surprise there.

<u>Drinking Too Much Alcohol is Bad for You</u>

1) Being <u>DRUNK</u> is a <u>SHORT-TERM EFFECT</u> of drinking too much <u>alcohol</u>.
   It causes:

<u>blurred</u> vision

<u>slurred</u> speech

bad <u>judgement</u>

bad <u>muscle control</u>

lots of blood
<u>flow to the skin</u>

sleepiness

rubbish <u>balance</u>

2) <u>BRAIN</u> and <u>LIVER DAMAGE</u> are <u>LONG-TERM EFFECTS</u> of drinking too much alcohol.

3) Doctors say you shouldn't drink more than:

<u>21 UNITS OF ALCOHOL</u>
a week if you're a <u>MAN</u>.

<u>14 UNITS</u> a week if
you're a <u>WOMAN</u>.

<u>1 unit</u> =
- half a pint of beer
- 1 small glass of wine

<u>You're Not Allowed to Drive When You're Drunk</u>

(1) You're <u>NOT ALLOWED</u> to <u>DRIVE</u> or fly a <u>PLANE</u> when you're <u>DRUNK</u>.

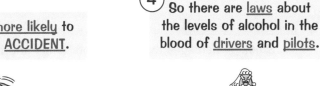

(2) This is because your
<u>REACTION TIME</u> is
<u>SLOWER</u> when you <u>drink</u>.

(3) You're <u>more likely</u> to
have an <u>ACCIDENT</u>.

(4) So there are <u>laws</u> about
the levels of alcohol in the
blood of <u>drivers</u> and <u>pilots</u>.

Your reaction time is how long it takes
you to react to something you see or hear.

<u>Practice Questions</u>

1) Give <u>three</u> things that being <u>drunk</u> causes.
2) "Doctors say <u>men</u> shouldn't drink more than <u>14 units of alcohol</u> a week." True or false?
3) Why are you not allowed to <u>fly a plane</u> if you're drunk?

Smoking

There's nothing nice about smoking. It stinks and does bad things to your body. It can even kill you.

Burning Cigarettes Make Four Main Things:

1. CARBON MONOXIDE	2. NICOTINE	3. PARTICULATES	4. TAR
Makes the <u>blood</u> carry <u>less oxygen</u>. This can lead to <u>heart disease</u>.	Makes <u>smoking addictive</u>.	Tiny <u>bits of dust</u> that build up in the lungs. They cause <u>irritation</u> (soreness).	Causes <u>irritation</u>.

Must have cigarette...

Tar also has chemicals in it that cause <u>cancer</u>. These are called <u>carcinogens</u>.

Smoking Causes All Sorts of Illnesses

Smoking causes:

(1) <u>HEART DISEASE</u>
(see page 8)

(2) <u>CANCER</u> of the:

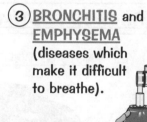

mouth

<u>oesophagus</u>
(food pipe)

<u>throat</u>

<u>lung</u>

(3) <u>BRONCHITIS</u> and <u>EMPHYSEMA</u>
(diseases which make it difficult to breathe).

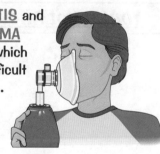

(4) <u>SMOKER'S COUGH</u>
- Smoking damages the <u>cilia</u> in your lungs and throat.
- The damaged cilia <u>can't get rid of mucus</u>.
- The mucus <u>sticks</u> in your lungs.
- This makes you <u>cough more</u>.

Cilia are tiny hairs.

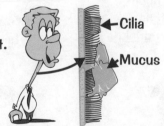

←Cilia

←Mucus

Practice Questions

1) Name <u>four</u> things made by burning cigarettes.
2) Tar has <u>chemicals</u> in it that <u>cause cancer</u>. What are these chemicals called?
3) Smoking causes different <u>illness</u>. Name <u>three</u> of these illnesses.

Module B1 — Understanding Ourselves

The Eye

Your eyes are pretty <u>important</u>. You need them to read this page for a start.

Learn the Eye with All Its Labels:

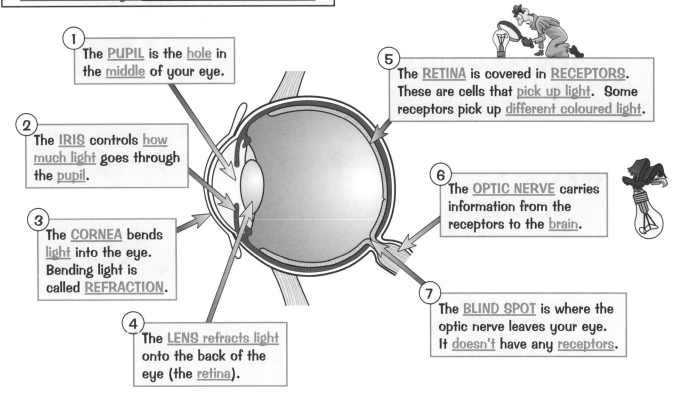

① The <u>PUPIL</u> is the <u>hole</u> in the <u>middle</u> of your eye.

② The <u>IRIS</u> controls <u>how much light</u> goes through the <u>pupil</u>.

③ The <u>CORNEA</u> bends <u>light</u> into the eye. Bending light is called <u>REFRACTION</u>.

④ The <u>LENS refracts light</u> onto the back of the eye (the <u>retina</u>).

⑤ The <u>RETINA</u> is covered in <u>RECEPTORS</u>. These are cells that <u>pick up light</u>. Some receptors pick up <u>different coloured light</u>.

⑥ The <u>OPTIC NERVE</u> carries information from the receptors to the <u>brain</u>.

⑦ The <u>BLIND SPOT</u> is where the optic nerve leaves your eye. It <u>doesn't</u> have any <u>receptors</u>.

The Light Travels Through the Eye like This...

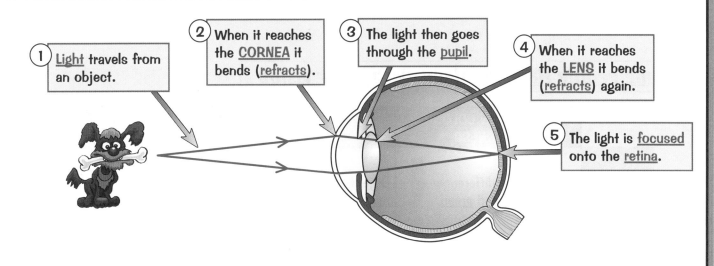

① <u>Light</u> travels from an object.

② When it reaches the <u>CORNEA</u> it bends (<u>refracts</u>).

③ The light then goes through the <u>pupil</u>.

④ When it reaches the <u>LENS</u> it bends (<u>refracts</u>) again.

⑤ The light is <u>focused</u> onto the <u>retina</u>.

Practice Questions

1) What does the <u>iris</u> do?
2) What part of the eye carries <u>information</u> to the <u>brain</u>?
3) Name <u>two</u> parts of the eye that <u>refract light</u>.

Vision

This page is all about how different animals <u>see</u>.

Some Animals Have Binocular Vision

1) Animals with <u>binocular vision</u> have <u>eyes</u> on the <u>FRONT</u> of their <u>head</u>.

2) This lets the animals <u>tell how far away</u> something is.
This is called being able to <u>JUDGE DISTANCES</u>.

3) Here's how they do it:

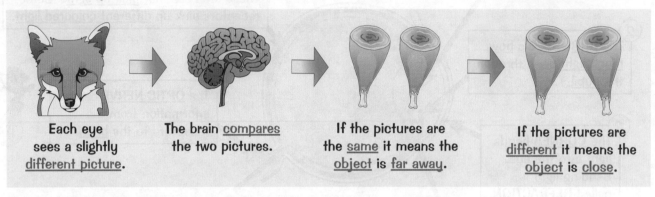

| Each eye sees a slightly <u>different picture</u>. | The brain <u>compares</u> the two pictures. | If the pictures are the <u>same</u> it means the <u>object</u> is <u>far away</u>. | If the pictures are <u>different</u> it means the <u>object</u> is <u>close</u>. |

4) But having binocular vision means you <u>can't see very far</u> to the <u>left</u> or <u>right</u>.
This is called having a <u>NARROW FIELD OF VISION</u>.

Other Animals Have Monocular Vision

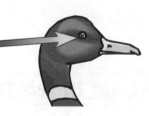

1) Animals with <u>MONOCULAR VISION</u> have <u>eyes</u> on the <u>SIDES</u> of their <u>head</u>.

2) This gives an animal a <u>WIDE FIELD OF VISION</u>.
This means the animal can see <u>a long way</u> to the <u>left</u> and <u>right</u>.

3) But animals with monocular vision <u>CAN'T JUDGE DISTANCES</u>.

Some People Have Problems With Their Vision

	RED-GREEN COLOUR BLINDNESS	LONG-SIGHTEDNESS	SHORT-SIGHTEDNESS
Problem:	Can't tell the difference between <u>red</u> and <u>green</u>.	Objects that are <u>nearby</u> look blurry.	Objects that are <u>far away</u> look blurry.
Cause:	Special <u>receptors</u> in the retina are <u>missing</u>.	<u>Lens</u> or the <u>eyeball</u> is the <u>wrong shape</u>.	<u>Lens</u> or the <u>eyeball</u> is the <u>wrong shape</u>.

Practice Questions

1) What does having <u>binocular vision</u> let animals do?

2) What causes <u>red-green colour blindness</u>?

Neurones

Neurones are <u>really long cells</u> that go all over your body. You've got millions of them.

Neurones Carry Information Around the Body

1) <u>Neurones</u> are nerve cells. They look like this:

2) Neurones carry <u>information</u>.

3) This information is sent as <u>NERVE IMPULSES</u>.

4) A nerve impulse is an <u>ELECTRICAL SIGNAL</u>. It travels along the <u>AXON</u> of the neurone.

5) Nerve impulses are very <u>FAST</u>.

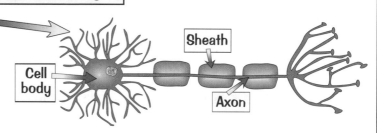

Sheath

Cell body

Axon

Your Nervous System Has Two Main Bits

1) The <u>CENTRAL NERVOUS SYSTEM</u> is the <u>BRAIN</u> and <u>SPINAL CORD</u>. It's sometimes called the <u>CNS</u> for short.

2) All the neurones that <u>aren't in</u> the <u>brain</u> or <u>spinal cord</u> are part of the <u>PERIPHERAL NERVOUS SYSTEM</u>.

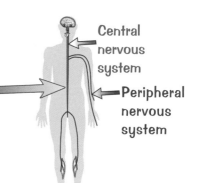

Central nervous system

Peripheral nervous system

The Central Nervous System Sorts Out Information

1) The central nervous system <u>sorts out information</u>. Here's how:

① There's a <u>STIMULUS</u>. A stimulus is a <u>change</u> in the <u>environment</u>. For example, a <u>killer mummy</u> appears.

② <u>RECEPTORS</u> — pick up the <u>stimulus</u>.

③ <u>CNS</u> — <u>decides</u> what to do about the stimulus.

④ <u>EFFECTORS</u> — follow instructions from the CNS. Effectors are <u>MUSCLES</u> and <u>GLANDS</u>.

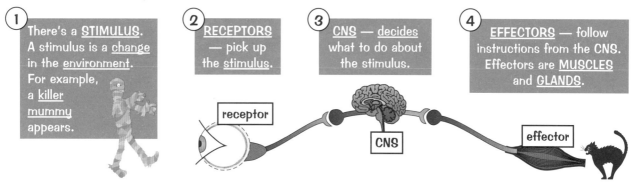

receptor

CNS

effector

2) There are <u>THREE TYPES of neurone</u> — <u>SENSORY</u> neurones, <u>RELAY</u> neurones and <u>MOTOR</u> neurones.

3) The <u>neurones</u> in the central nervous system <u>work</u> like this:

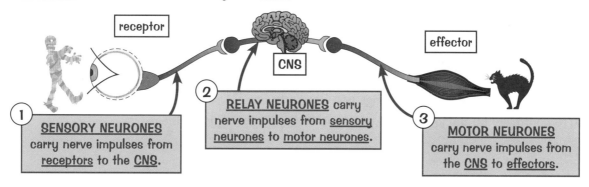

receptor

CNS

effector

① <u>SENSORY NEURONES</u> carry nerve impulses from <u>receptors</u> to the <u>CNS</u>.

② <u>RELAY NEURONES</u> carry nerve impulses from <u>sensory neurones</u> to <u>motor neurones</u>.

③ <u>MOTOR NEURONES</u> carry nerve impulses from the <u>CNS</u> to <u>effectors</u>.

Practice Questions

1) What is a <u>nerve impulse</u>?

2) What is the <u>central nervous system</u>?

Reflexes

The reflex. It might just save your life one day.

Reflexes Stop You Hurting Yourself

1) A REFLEX is an action that stops you hurting yourself.

2) Reflexes are AUTOMATIC. This means you DON'T HAVE TO THINK about doing them.

3) Reflexes are also very FAST.

4) The BRAIN DOESN'T usually control reflexes. Nerve impulses travel through the spinal cord instead.

5) Pulling back your hand when you touch a hot plate is a reflex. It stops you burning your hand.

   This is how it works:

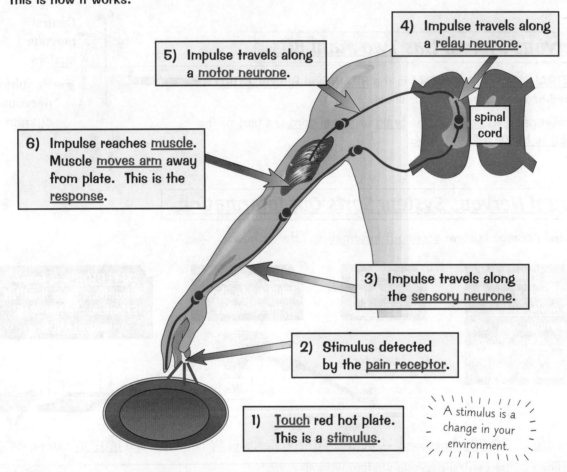

4) Impulse travels along a relay neurone.

5) Impulse travels along a motor neurone.

spinal cord

6) Impulse reaches muscle. Muscle moves arm away from plate. This is the response.

3) Impulse travels along the sensory neurone.

2) Stimulus detected by the pain receptor.

1) Touch red hot plate. This is a stimulus.

A stimulus is a change in your environment.

Voluntary Responses are Different from Reflexes

1) VOLUNTARY RESPONSES are the things you decide to do.

2) They're controlled by the brain — so you have to THINK about doing them.

Practice Questions

1) What is a reflex?

2) "Reflexes are automatic." What does this mean?

3) "Reflexes are slow." True or false?

Module B1 — Understanding Ourselves

Homeostasis

Homeostasis — it sounds scary, but it's not too bad. Honest.

Homeostasis Keeps the Conditions Inside Your Body the Same

1) Homeostasis means keeping conditions inside your body the same.
This is called maintaining a CONSTANT INTERNAL ENVIRONMENT.

2) The conditions in your body need to be kept the same so that your CELLS can work properly.

3) Water level, body temperature and carbon dioxide level are all kept the same by homeostasis.

Enzymes speed up chemical reactions in the body.

Core Body Temperature is 37 °C

1) The enzymes in your body work best at 37 °C. So your body needs to stay at 37 °C.

2) Your body does these things to stay at this temperature:

When You're TOO HOT:

1) You SWEAT. When sweat EVAPORATES it takes heat from your skin. This cools you down.

2) MORE BLOOD flows near the SURFACE of the SKIN. So you lose more heat.

'Evaporates' is when a liquid becomes a gas.

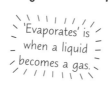

If you get too hot you can get DEHYDRATED and HEAT STROKE. These can kill you.

When You're TOO COLD:

1) You DON'T SWEAT.

2) LESS BLOOD flows near the SURFACE of the SKIN. So you lose less heat.

3) SHIVERING and EXERCISING can keep you warm.

4) You can add EXTRA CLOTHES.

If you get too cold you can get HYPOTHERMIA. This can kill you.

You can Measure Body Temperature in Different Ways

1) You can measure the temperature of your ear, finger, mouth or anus (bum).

2) To measure your temperature you can use:

CLINICAL THERMOMETERS

TEMPERATURE-SENSITIVE STRIPS

DIGITAL THERMOMETERS

THERMAL IMAGING

©iStockphoto.com/-Vladimir-

Practice Questions

1) Name three things kept the same by homeostasis.

2) Give two things the body does when it gets too hot.

3) Give one thing you can use to measure your body temperature.

Hormones and Controlling Blood Sugar

The <u>amount</u> of <u>sugar</u> in your <u>blood</u> is <u>controlled</u> by <u>homeostasis</u>. Learn how it works.

Your Blood Sugar Level Needs to be Controlled

1) Your <u>blood sugar level</u> is the <u>amount of sugar</u> in your <u>blood</u>.

2) Eating <u>carbohydrates</u> will <u>INCREASE</u> your blood sugar level.

3) <u>Respiration</u> will <u>DECREASE</u> your blood sugar level.

4) Your blood sugar level is <u>controlled</u> by <u>INSULIN</u>. Insulin is a <u>HORMONE</u>.

5) Insulin is <u>produced</u> by an organ called the <u>PANCREAS</u>.

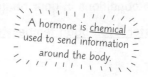
A hormone is <u>chemical</u> used to send information around the body.

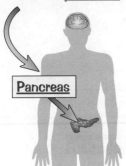
Pancreas

Here's how insulin controls the blood sugar level:

Blood sugar level too high.

Pancreas adds insulin to the blood.
insulin

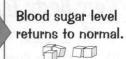
Blood sugar level returns to normal.

Hormones Travel in the Blood

1) Insulin <u>travels</u> around the body in the <u>BLOOD</u>. Other <u>hormones</u> also travel in the blood.

2) Each hormone only affects <u>SOME</u> organs. These are called <u>TARGET ORGANS</u>.

3) Travelling by blood is <u>SLOW</u>. So the body reacts to hormones <u>more slowly</u> than it does to nerve impulses.

Nerve impulses are <u>fast</u>.
See page 19.

Having Diabetes Means You Can't Control Your Blood Sugar Level

People with diabetes <u>can't control their blood sugar level</u>. There are <u>TWO types</u> of diabetes:

TYPE 1 DIABETES	TYPE 2 DIABETES
Type 1 diabetes is where the <u>pancreas CAN'T PRODUCE INSULIN</u>. 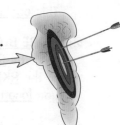 no insulin	Type 2 diabetes is where a person <u>CAN'T REACT to INSULIN</u>. insulin BUT... Blood sugar level stays high.
It can be controlled by <u>injecting</u> <u>insulin</u> into the blood.	It's normally controlled by <u>avoiding sugary foods</u>.

Practice Questions

1) Name the <u>hormone</u> that controls the <u>amount</u> of <u>sugar</u> in the <u>blood</u>.

2) How do hormones <u>travel</u> around the body?

Plant Hormones and Growth

Just like animals, plants <u>respond</u> to changes in their <u>environment</u>. They do this by <u>growing</u>.

Auxins are Plant Growth Hormones

1) How <u>plants grow</u> is controlled by <u>PLANT GROWTH HORMONES</u>.

2) <u>AUXINS</u> are a type of plant growth hormone.

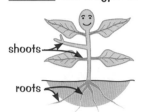

shoots

roots

Auxins control how <u>ROOTS</u> and <u>SHOOTS</u> grow.

Auxins <u>move</u> around the plant in <u>water</u>. The posh way of saying this is that '<u>auxins move through the plant in SOLUTION</u>'.

3) Other plant growth hormones control when <u>FRUIT</u> becomes <u>RIPE</u> and when <u>FLOWERS GROW</u>.

Auxins Change the Direction of Root and Shoot Growth

Auxins make <u>shoots</u> <u>grow towards light</u>.

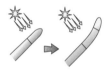

This is <u>POSITIVE PHOTOTROPISM</u>.

Auxins make <u>shoots</u> <u>grow away from gravity</u>.

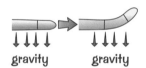

gravity   gravity

This is <u>NEGATIVE GEOTROPISM</u>.

Auxins make <u>roots</u> <u>grow away from light</u>.

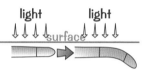

light   light

surface

This is <u>NEGATIVE PHOTOTROPISM</u>.

Auxins make <u>roots</u> <u>grow towards gravity</u>.

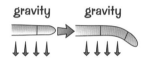

gravity   gravity

This is <u>POSITIVE GEOTROPISM</u>.

1) Plants <u>need LIGHT</u> for <u>PHOTOSYNTHESIS</u>. This is how they make their <u>FOOD</u>.
2) If plants don't get enough light, they <u>die</u>.
3) So plant <u>shoots grow towards the light</u> to <u>SURVIVE</u>.
4) Plants also need <u>water</u>. Plant <u>roots grow downwards</u> to reach water in the <u>soil</u>.

This Experiment Shows That Shoots Grow Towards Light

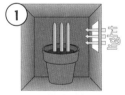

Put a plant inside a <u>cardboard box</u> with a <u>hole</u> in <u>one</u> side.

Leave the plant for a <u>few days</u>. The shoots will start to bend and <u>grow towards the light</u>.

You also need a <u>CONTROL EXPERIMENT</u>. This should be a plant <u>surrounded by light</u> on all sides. The plant <u>shouldn't bend</u>.

The control experiment is used to show that light is the only thing making the plant bend.

Practice Questions

1) What are <u>auxins</u>?
2) "Shoots show <u>positive geotropism</u>." True or false?

Commercial Uses of Plant Hormones

> Plant hormones can be used to SPEED UP or SLOW DOWN plant growth.

This means plant hormones have lots of uses...

1) As *Selective Weedkillers*

Weeds

Groovy

SELECTIVE WEEDKILLERS are plant growth hormones. They only affect WEEDS.

The weedkillers stop the weeds growing. This kills them.

Grass and crops aren't affected by these weedkillers.

2) *Growing from Cuttings with Rooting Powder*

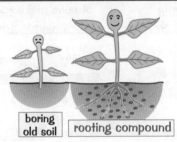
boring old soil | rooting compound

1) A CUTTING is part of a plant that has been cut off. For example, the end of a branch with a few leaves on it.

2) If you stick a cutting in the soil and add ROOTING POWDER, it will grow roots quickly.

3) The cutting will then grow into a new plant.

4) This is because rooting powder contains growth hormones.

3) *Controlling the Ripening of Fruit*

1) Plant hormones can make fruit ripen more SLOWLY.

2) They can also make fruit ripen more QUICKLY.

3) So plant hormones can be used to make sure fruit is ripe by the time it gets to the shops.

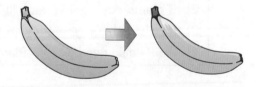

4) *Controlling Dormancy*

1) Some seeds won't start growing until they've been through certain conditions. For example, cold conditions. This is called DORMANCY.

2) Plant hormones can STOP dormancy and make seeds START GROWING.

Practice Questions

1) What are selective weedkillers?

2) "Rooting powder contains plant hormones." True or false?

3) How could you stop dormancy?

Genes and Chromosomes

This stuff looks more tricky than it really is. Honest. In fact, it's pretty <u>interesting</u>.

1) Most cells in your body have a <u>NUCLEUS</u>. The nucleus has <u>CHROMOSOMES</u> in it.

2) Chromosomes come in <u>PAIRS</u>.
- Different species have a different <u>number of pairs</u>.
- Humans have <u>23 pairs</u> of <u>chromosomes</u> in each body cell.

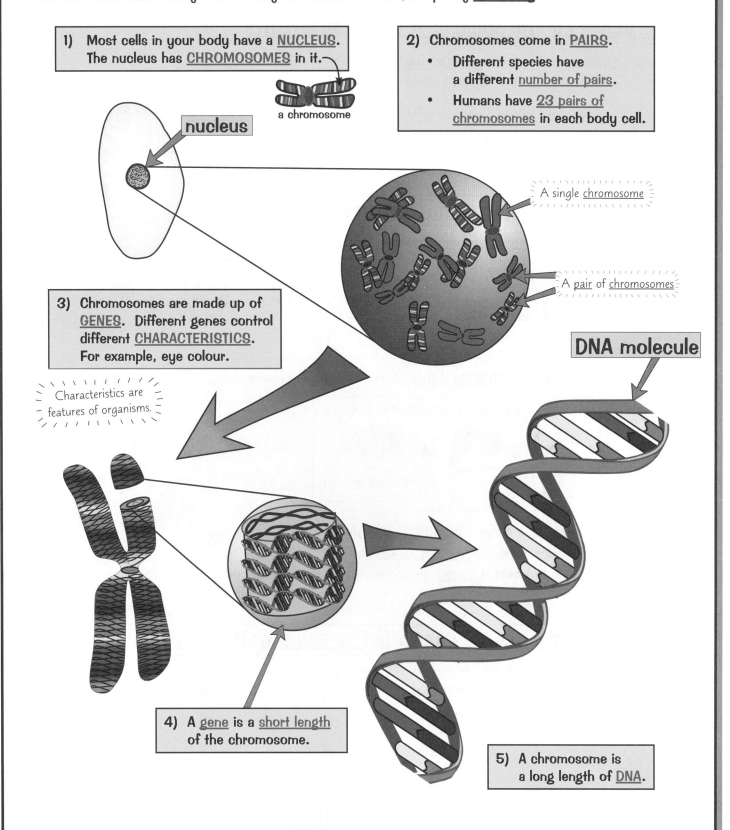

a chromosome

nucleus

A single <u>chromosome</u>

A <u>pair</u> of <u>chromosomes</u>

3) Chromosomes are made up of <u>GENES</u>. Different genes control different <u>CHARACTERISTICS</u>. For example, eye colour.

Characteristics are features of organisms.

DNA molecule

4) A <u>gene</u> is a <u>short length</u> of the chromosome.

5) A chromosome is a long length of <u>DNA</u>.

Practice Questions

1) Where in your cells are the <u>chromosomes</u> found?

2) How many <u>pairs of chromosomes</u> does a human body cell have?

3) What do <u>genes</u> control?

Module B1 — Understanding Ourselves

Genes and the Environment

Your characteristics are down to your genes and your environment.

Your Genes Control Some of Your Characteristics

1) Your GENES control some of your CHARACTERISTICS. For example, eye colour.

2) There can be DIFFERENT VERSIONS of the SAME GENE. These are called ALLELES.

For example, you could have an allele for blue eyes or an allele for brown eyes.

3) Everybody has a different set of alleles — this is called GENETIC VARIATION.

You Can Inherit These Characteristics

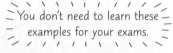
You don't need to learn these examples for your exams.

1) You can INHERIT (get) characteristics from your parents. For example:

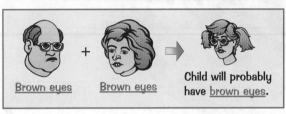

Brown eyes + Brown eyes → Child will probably have brown eyes.

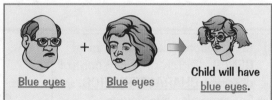

Blue eyes + Blue eyes → Child will have blue eyes.

2) Some characteristics are STRONGER than others though. For example:

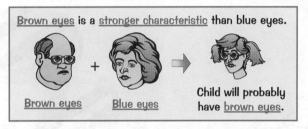

Brown eyes is a stronger characteristic than blue eyes.

Brown eyes + Blue eyes → Child will probably have brown eyes.

3) Strong characteristics are called DOMINANT CHARACTERISTICS.

4) Weak characteristics are called RECESSIVE CHARACTERISTICS.

5) You're more likely to inherit dominant characteristics than recessive ones.

Most Characteristics are Controlled by Genes and Environment

1) Not all of your characteristics are controlled by your genes.

2) Some are controlled by your ENVIRONMENT. For example, you can get scars from accidents.

3) But most of your characteristics are controlled by your genes AND your environment. For example:

INTELLIGENCE
Some of your genes could make you clever. But not if you don't study.

BODY MASS
Your genes affect your weight. But your weight will change if you diet or eat too much.

HEIGHT
If you have tall parents, you're likely to be tall too. But only if you eat enough when you're growing.

Practice Questions

1) What are alleles?

2) Give one characteristic that's controlled by both your genes and your environment.

Gametes and Genetic Variation

Everyone (except identical twins) has <u>different genes</u> to everyone else. This page is all about why...

Gametes are Sperm Cells and Egg Cells

1) GAMETES are SPERM and EGG cells.

2) Normal <u>body cells</u> have <u>46 chromosomes</u>. These chromosomes come in <u>PAIRS</u>.

3) <u>Gametes</u> have <u>23 chromosomes</u>. That's <u>HALF</u> the number of chromosomes in normal body cells.

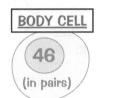

There are Three Things That Cause Genetic Variation

① Making Gametes

1) Gametes are made from <u>body cells</u>.

2) To make a gamete, a body cell <u>splits in two</u>.

3) The <u>chromosome pairs SPLIT UP</u>. <u>ONE</u> chromosome from each pair goes into each <u>gamete</u>.

4) Each gamete ends up with a <u>MIXTURE of chromosomes</u>.

5) This causes <u>genetic variation</u>.

② Fertilisation — the Gametes Join Together

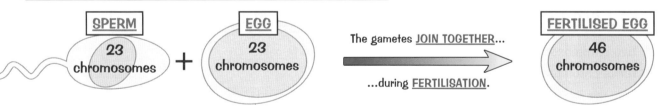

The gametes JOIN TOGETHER...

...during FERTILISATION.

1) <u>FERTILISATION</u> is when the <u>sperm</u> and the <u>egg</u> join to make a new cell.

2) Fertilisation is <u>RANDOM</u> — you don't know which two gametes are going to join together.

3) This causes <u>genetic variation</u>.

③ Mutations — Changes to Genes

1) Sometimes a gene <u>MUTATES</u>. This just means that the gene <u>changes</u>.

2) This can create <u>new characteristics</u>, which <u>increases genetic variation</u>.

Practice Questions

1) How many <u>chromosomes</u> are found in <u>human gametes</u>?

2) What is <u>fertilisation</u>?

Genetic Disorders and Sex Inheritance

There's been <u>a lot to learn</u> about genes. This is the last page though, I promise.

Genetic Disorders are Caused by Faulty Genes

<u>Genetic disorders</u> are <u>illnesses</u>. They're caused by <u>faulty genes</u>. These are genes that <u>don't work</u> properly. Here are some <u>examples</u> of genetic disorders:

CYSTIC FIBROSIS	RED-GREEN COLOUR BLINDNESS	SICKLE CELL ANAEMIA
The body makes a lot of thick, sticky <u>mucus</u> in the <u>airways</u> and <u>pancreas</u>.	It's hard to tell the <u>difference</u> between <u>red</u> and <u>green</u>.	The <u>red blood cells</u> are the <u>wrong shape</u>.

Knowing There are Genetic Disorders in Your Family Can Be Difficult

If you find out there's a <u>genetic disorder</u> in your <u>family</u>, you might face some <u>hard questions</u>:

Your Chromosomes Control Whether You're Male or Female

1) Two chromosomes decide whether you turn out <u>male</u> or <u>female</u>.
2) These chromosomes are labelled <u>X</u> and <u>Y</u>.

- <u>All women</u> have <u>two X chromosomes</u>: XX
- The <u>XX combination</u> causes <u>female characteristics</u>.

- <u>All men</u> have an <u>X</u> and a <u>Y</u> chromosome: XY
- The <u>Y chromosome</u> causes <u>male characteristics</u>.

3) This happens in <u>all mammals</u>, but not in plants.

Practice Questions

1) What is <u>cystic fibrosis</u>?
2) Suggest <u>one question</u> you might ask if you knew you had a <u>genetic disease</u> in your family.
3) What chromosome combinations make someone: a) <u>female</u> b) <u>male</u>?

Atoms, Molecules and Compounds

Everything is made up of atoms. They're really, really tiny.

Atoms have a Nucleus And Electrons

1) The NUCLEUS is in the middle of the atom.
2) The ELECTRONS move round the nucleus.
   Electrons are NEGATIVE (−).

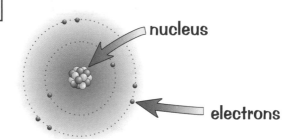

Atoms Are Joined Together by Bonds

Atoms can be joined together by their electrons. This is called a chemical bond. There are two sorts...

...COVALENT Bonds

1) In a covalent bond atoms SHARE a PAIR of electrons.
2) This holds them together.

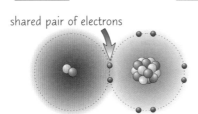

shared pair of electrons

...Or IONIC Bonds

1) Sometimes atoms can LOSE or get EXTRA electrons.
2) When this happens they're called IONS.

It's easy to spot ions, they've all got a + or − sign.

This atom GIVES AWAY an electron. It becomes a POSITIVE (+) ion.

This atom TAKES the electron. It becomes a NEGATIVE (−) ion.

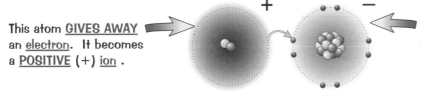

3) POSITIVE ions attract NEGATIVE ions.
4) This is attraction is called an IONIC BOND. It holds the atoms together.

(a bit like with magnets)

Joined-Up Atoms Are Called Molecules

1) One way to show atoms is as a BLOB with a letter in. For example, ⓞ shows one atom.
2) The letter tells you what SORT of atom it is. ⓞ = an OXYGEN atom.
3) Atoms joined together make MOLECULES: ⓞⓞ = an oxygen MOLECULE.
4) If the atoms in a molecule are the SAME it's called an ELEMENT. So oxygen ⓞⓞ is an element.
5) If the atoms in a molecule are DIFFERENT it's called a COMPOUND.
6) For example, carbon dioxide has one CARBON atom and two OXYGEN atoms. ⓞⒸⓞ So it's a compound.

Practice Questions

1) Are electrons positive or negative?
2) What is a molecule made of?
3) Sometimes atoms share a pair of electrons. What type of bond is this?

Chemical Formulas

Formulas are a quick way to write chemicals — they save you from writing out the whole name.

There are TWO SORTS of Formula

1 Molecular Formulas

These show you WHAT KIND of atoms there are and HOW MANY there are.
For example, the molecular formula of carbon dioxide is CO_2.

The C means there is a CARBON atom.

CO_2

The O means there is an OXYGEN atom.

The 2 after the O means there are TWO of the O atoms.

Carbon dioxide

2 Displayed Formulas

These show you the atoms and the BONDS between them.
For example, the displayed formula of water is:

Water has two bonds.
(Bonds are shown by lines.)

H—O—H

2 hydrogen (H) atoms.

1 oxygen (O) atom.

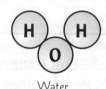
Water

You Can Swap from a Displayed Formula to a Molecular Formula

DISPLAYED formula	What it shows	MOLECULAR formula
Cl-Cl	two chlorine atoms	Cl_2
H H-C-H H	one carbon atom and four hydrogen atoms	CH_4

Some Molecular Formulas Have Brackets

1) If the molecular formula has brackets in it you can still work out what atoms you've got.
   For example, the molecular formula of calcium hydroxide is $Ca(OH)_2$:

$$Ca(OH)_2$$

The 2 after the bracket means there are 2 lots of OH.

2) Write it out without the brackets: **CaOHOH**

3) Count up the atoms. **1 Calcium, 2 Oxygen, 2 Hydrogen**

Practice Questions

1) How many carbon atoms are there in CO_2?
2) Write the molecular formula from this displayed formula.
3) How many oxygen atoms are there in $Mg(OH)_2$?

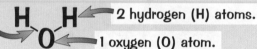

H   H
| |
H-C-C-H
| |
H   H

Chemical Equations

Chemical equations are a quick way of writing what goes on in a chemical reaction.

Chemical Equations Show What Happens in a Reaction

1) In a chemical reaction chemicals REACT together to make NEW chemicals.

2) For example, when sodium and water react you get sodium hydroxide and hydrogen.

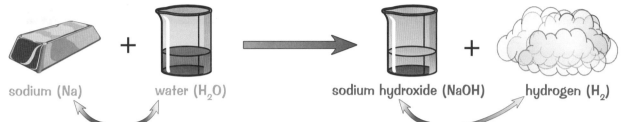

sodium (Na)　　+　　water (H_2O)　→　sodium hydroxide (NaOH)　+　hydrogen (H_2)

3) The chemicals that react are called REACTANTS. The chemicals that are made are called PRODUCTS.

4) You can write out a chemical reaction using words or molecular formulas. For example...

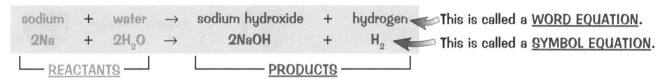

sodium + water → sodium hydroxide + hydrogen — This is called a WORD EQUATION.
$2Na$ + $2H_2O$ → $2NaOH$ + H_2 — This is called a SYMBOL EQUATION.
└── REACTANTS ──┘　　└── PRODUCTS ──┘

Symbol Equations Need to be Balanced

1) For a symbol equation to be right it has to be BALANCED.

2) This means it has to have the SAME NUMBER of each type of atom on each side of the arrow.

3) You balance equations by putting numbers in front of the molecules. For example:

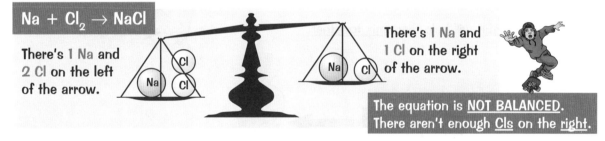

$Na + Cl_2 \rightarrow NaCl$

There's 1 Na and 2 Cl on the left of the arrow.

There's 1 Na and 1 Cl on the right of the arrow.

The equation is NOT BALANCED. There aren't enough Cls on the right.

To balance the equation, put a 2 in front of the NaCl and a 2 in front of the Na.

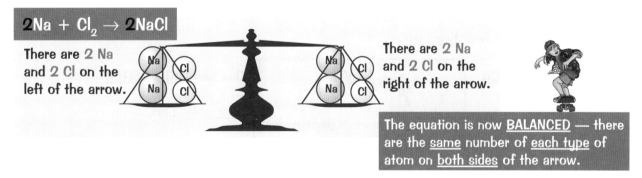

$2Na + Cl_2 \rightarrow 2NaCl$

There are 2 Na and 2 Cl on the left of the arrow.

There are 2 Na and 2 Cl on the right of the arrow.

The equation is now BALANCED — there are the same number of each type of atom on both sides of the arrow.

Practice Questions

1) What are the reactants in this reaction: hydrogen + oxygen → water

2) Is this equation balanced? $H_2 + O_2 \rightarrow H_2O$

3) Is this equation balanced? $2H_2 + O_2 \rightarrow 2H_2O$

Food Additives

Additives are things that are added to <u>food</u>. Additives stop food <u>going off</u> and make it <u>look</u> and <u>taste better</u>.

Additives <u>Are Chemicals</u> Added to Food

1) <u>Additives</u> are <u>chemicals</u> that are added to food to <u>IMPROVE it</u>.

2) <u>Food colours</u>, <u>flavour enhancers</u> and <u>antioxidants</u> are all additives.

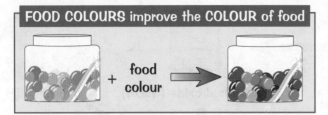

FOOD COLOURS improve the COLOUR of food

+ food colour

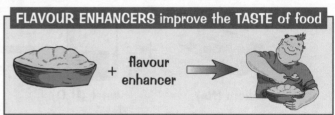

FLAVOUR ENHANCERS improve the TASTE of food

+ flavour enhancer

ANTIOXIDANTS stop food REACTING with OXYGEN

1) When some foods react with <u>OXYGEN</u> in the air, they <u>go off</u>.

2) For example, <u>slices of apple</u> go <u>brown</u> because they react with the air.

3) <u>Antioxidants</u> are added to foods to <u>STOP</u> this happening.

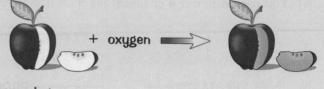

+ oxygen

Emulsifiers <u>Are a Type of</u> Additive

1) <u>Oil</u> and <u>water</u> don't normally <u>mix</u> — they <u>SEPARATE</u> into two layers.

2) Adding an <u>EMULSIFIER</u> will help them <u>mix together</u>.

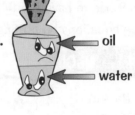

oil

water

+ EMULSIFIER →

3) <u>Emulsifier molecules</u> have <u>two parts</u>:

One part <u>LIKES OIL</u> — it's called the <u>hydrophobic</u> part.

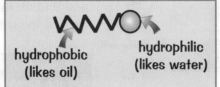

hydrophobic (likes oil)

hydrophilic (likes water)

One part <u>LIKES WATER</u> — it's called the <u>hydrophilic</u> part.

Practice Questions

1) Does the <u>hydrophobic</u> part of an emulsifier molecule like <u>oil</u> or <u>water</u>?

2) Antioxidants are food additives. Name two <u>other</u> types of <u>food additive</u>.

3) <u>Antioxidants</u> are sometimes added to food. What do they do?

Cooking and Chemical Change

When you cook things, the chemicals in the food change, and they can't change back. Here's why.

Cooking Causes Chemical Changes

1) Cooking food needs ENERGY (heat).
2) Cooking causes a CHEMICAL change. This means new substances are made.

raw meat   HEAT   cooked meat   raw egg   HEAT   cooked egg

3) Cooking is IRREVERSIBLE.
4) This means that once you've cooked something, you can't change it back.
5) When meat and eggs are cooked the protein molecules in the food CHANGE SHAPE.
6) This is called DENATURING.

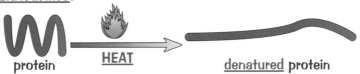

protein   HEAT   denatured protein

Baking Powder Breaks Down When Heated

1) Baking powder is used in baking cakes.
2) It has a chemical called SODIUM HYDROGENCARBONATE in it.
3) When it's HEATED the sodium hydrogencarbonate splits up.
4) Sodium carbonate, carbon dioxide and water are made.

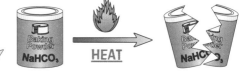

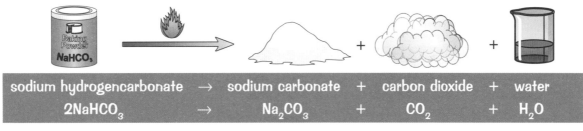

sodium hydrogencarbonate	→	sodium carbonate	+	carbon dioxide	+	water
$2NaHCO_3$	→	Na_2CO_3	+	CO_2	+	H_2O

5) The carbon dioxide makes the cake RISE.

+ CO_2

6) You can test for carbon dioxide by bubbling it through LIMEWATER. It'll make the limewater go CLOUDY.

CO_2 gas

Limewater   Cloudy limewater

Practice Questions

1)   What is it called when protein molecules are cooked and change shape?
2)   What gas is made when baking powder is heated?

Perfumes

Some things smell nice, some don't... it's all down to <u>chemicals</u>.

Make-up And Perfume Are Cosmetics

<u>Cosmetics</u> can be natural or synthetic.

 1) <u>NATURAL</u> cosmetics come from <u>natural SOURCES</u> like flowers.

A source is where something comes from.

 2) <u>SYNTHETIC</u> cosmetics are <u>made</u> in a lab.

Esters Are Used as Perfumes

1) Esters are <u>made</u> by reacting an <u>ACID</u> with an <u>ALCOHOL</u>. ➡️ Acid + Alcohol → Ester + Water

2) This is how to <u>make</u> an <u>ester</u>:

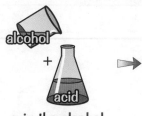
<u>mix</u> the <u>alcohol</u> and <u>acid</u>

<u>warm</u> gently

add <u>sodium carbonate</u>

smell carefully

Not All Chemicals Make Good Perfumes

1) To make a perfume, you need a <u>chemical</u> that has certain <u>PROPERTIES</u>.

2) A <u>property</u> of a chemical is <u>what it's like</u>. <u>PERFUMES</u> need to have <u>these</u> properties:

Evaporate means turn from liquid to gas.

Easily EVAPORATES — so the perfume will reach your <u>nose</u> and you will <u>smell it</u>.

Is NON-TOXIC — or it would <u>poison</u> you.

Doesn't REACT with WATER — or it would react with <u>sweat</u>.

Doesn't IRRITATE the SKIN — or you couldn't <u>wear it</u>.

Doesn't DISSOLVE in water — or it would <u>wash off</u>.

New Cosmetics Have to be Tested

1) New cosmetics are <u>TESTED</u> to make sure they are <u>SAFE</u> to use.

2) Some tests use <u>animals</u>, but this can be <u>painful</u> for the animals.

3) So testing cosmetics on <u>animals</u> is <u>BANNED</u> in the <u>European Union</u>.

Practice Questions

1) What is the name for something that is <u>made in a lab</u>?

2) Why must perfumes <u>not dissolve in water</u>?

3) What is the <u>missing word</u> in this reaction: ACID + ALCOHOL → _____ + WATER

Solutions

Solutions are everywhere. For example, sea water, coffee and your bubble bath are all solutions.

A Solution is a Mixture of Solvent and Solute

1) When you add a solid to a liquid sometimes the solid seems to disappear.
2) This is called DISSOLVING.
3) The thing that dissolves is called the SOLUTE.
4) The liquid it dissolves in is called the SOLVENT.
5) The mixture you end up with is called a SOLUTION.

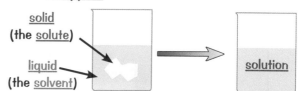

Only Soluble Things Dissolve

1) If something will dissolve then it's SOLUBLE.
2) If something won't dissolve then it's INSOLUBLE.

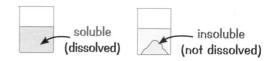

Different Solvents Are Better at Dissolving Different Things

1) You might get asked to choose which solvent you would use to dissolve something.
2) Here's a table showing how much of a solid dissolves in 100 g of three DIFFERENT solvents.

SOLVENT	How much SOLID dissolves?	Is the solvent EFFECTIVE? (GOOD at dissolving)
water	0 g	NO solid dissolves The solvent is NOT EFFECTIVE
nail varnish remover (acetone)	9.7 g	SOME solid dissolves The solvent is EFFECTIVE
ester (ethyl acetate)	25.0 g	LOTS of solid dissolves The solvent is VERY EFFECTIVE

Nail varnish remover dissolves nail varnish colours.

fruity smell waft

Practice Questions

1) Name two solvents.
2) What does insoluble mean?
3) What is the name for a mixture of a solute and a solvent?

Paints and Pigments

Lay down some <u>newspaper</u>, put on some <u>old clothes</u> and pick up a <u>brush</u>. It's <u>painting time</u>.

Paint is Made From a Pigment, a Binding Medium and a Solvent

1) <u>Paint</u> has three ingredients: <u>pigment</u>, <u>binding medium</u> and <u>solvent</u>.

INGREDIENT	WHAT IT DOES
pigment	Gives the paint its <u>COLOUR</u>
binding medium	<u>STICKS</u> the <u>pigment</u> to the <u>surface</u> you've painted
solvent	Makes the paint <u>THIN</u> and <u>easier to spread</u>

2) <u>Paint</u> is a <u>COLLOID</u>.

3) This means the <u>PIGMENT</u> particles are <u>mixed in</u> with the <u>LIQUID</u>, but <u>NOT dissolved</u>.

Another way of saying the particles are mixed in is saying they are <u>dispersed</u>.

Oil Paints And Emulsion Paints Are Different

1) The <u>binding medium</u> in paint is an <u>oil</u>.

2) The <u>solvent</u> in <u>OIL</u> paint is something that <u>DISSOLVES OIL</u>.

3) But the <u>solvent</u> in <u>EMULSION</u> paint is <u>WATER</u>.

Paints Dry When The Solvent Evaporates

1) <u>PAINT</u> is used to <u>decorate</u> and <u>protect</u> surfaces.

2) The <u>PAINT</u> goes on in a <u>thin layer</u>.

3) It <u>DRIES</u> as the solvent <u>evaporates</u> (turns from <u>liquid</u> to <u>gas</u>).

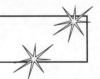

Practice Questions

1) What happens to paint when the <u>solvent evaporates</u>?

2) Which <u>ingredient</u> of paint <u>sticks</u> it to a surface?

3) What does <u>pigment</u> do in paint?

Module C1 — Carbon Chemistry

Special Pigments

If you thought <u>normal paint</u> was clever, wait till you read about the <u>pigments</u> on this page. They can <u>change colour</u> and even **glow in the dark**...

Thermochromic Pigments *Change Colour When Heated*

1) <u>Thermochromic pigments</u> are a special kind of pigment.

2) If you <u>HEAT</u> or <u>COOL</u> a <u>thermochromic pigment</u> it will <u>change colour</u>.

3) Here are three examples of how <u>thermochromic pigments</u> are used.

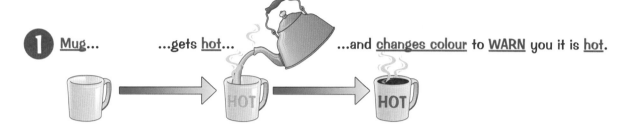

1 <u>Mug</u>... ...gets <u>hot</u>... ...and <u>changes colour</u> to <u>WARN</u> you it is <u>hot</u>.

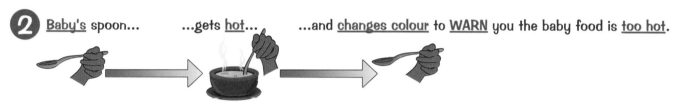

2 <u>Baby's</u> spoon... ...gets <u>hot</u>... ...and <u>changes colour</u> to <u>WARN</u> you the baby food is <u>too hot</u>.

3 <u>Mood ring</u>... ...<u>warms</u> up... ...and <u>CHANGES COLOUR</u>.

(And you thought it was all to do with how **calm** or how **passionate** you were...)

Phosphorescent Pigments *Glow in the Dark*

1) <u>Phosphorescent pigments</u> are another type of special pigment.

2) They're used in things like <u>glow-in-the-dark</u> clocks.

Phosphorescent pigments <u>ABSORB</u> (take in) <u>light energy</u>.

They <u>STORE</u> the light energy.

This energy is <u>released</u> as <u>light</u> over a period of time.

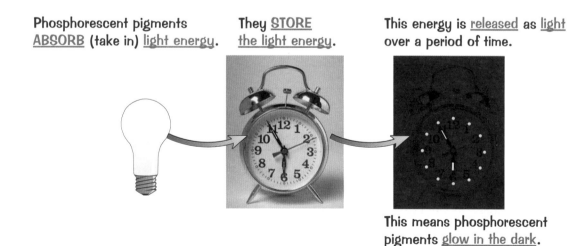

This means phosphorescent pigments <u>glow in the dark</u>.

Practice Questions

1) What happens to a thermochromic pigment if it is <u>heated</u>?

2) What do <u>phosphorescent</u> pigments do?

Polymers

Polymers are made of <u>lots</u> of molecules <u>joined together</u>...

Polymers are Made of Lots of Monomers

1) <u>Polymers</u> are <u>VERY LARGE</u> molecules.
2) Polymers are <u>made</u> when <u>LOTS OF SMALL MOLECULES</u> called <u>MONOMERS</u> join together.
3) This reaction is called <u>POLYMERISATION</u>.

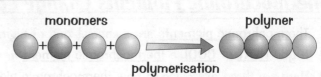

monomers   polymer

polymerisation

Alkenes are a Sort of Monomer

1) This is an <u>ALKENE</u>.
2) You can <u>join</u> alkene <u>monomers</u> together to make a <u>polymer</u>.
3) You need <u>HIGH PRESSURE</u> and a <u>CATALYST</u>.

A <u>catalyst</u> is a chemical that speeds up a reaction.

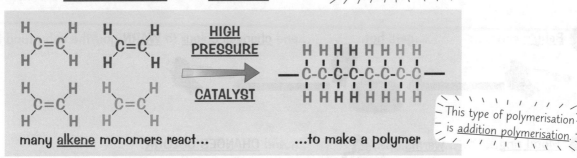

many <u>alkene</u> monomers react...   ...to make a polymer

This type of polymerisation is <u>addition polymerisation</u>.

Polymer Names Come From the Monomers They're Made From

To get the <u>name</u> of the <u>POLYMER</u>, put the word <u>"POLY"</u> in front of the <u>name</u> of the <u>MONOMER</u>. For example:

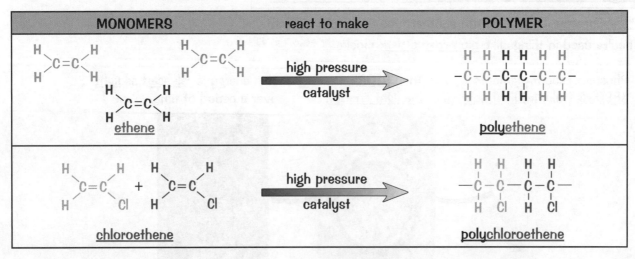

MONOMERS	react to make	POLYMER

To get the name of the <u>monomer</u> from the name of the <u>polymer</u> just <u>remove</u> the <u>POLY</u>.

Practice Questions

1) Is high or low <u>pressure</u> needed for a polymerisation reaction to happen?
2) <u>Polystyrene</u> is a polymer. What <u>monomer</u> is it made from?
3) What happens in a <u>polymerisation reaction</u>?

Polymers and Their Uses

Plastics are a type of polymer. They can be used to make all sorts of things.

What Polymers Are Used For Depends On Their Properties

1) Every material has different PROPERTIES.

2) Properties are what a material is LIKE. For example, polyethene is light and stretchy.

3) This makes it good for making plastic bags.

4) But it wouldn't be much good for making lunch boxes. You'd need a stiffer material like polypropene.

Polymers are Used to Make Clothes

NYLON and GORE-TEX® are used to make clothes. They are both:

1) WATERPROOF

2) Able to PROTECT against UV (ultraviolet) LIGHT

3) TOUGH

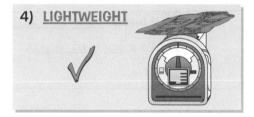

4) LIGHTWEIGHT

But Nylon Clothes Don't Let Water Escape

 NYLON is not breathable.

1) It doesn't let WATER VAPOUR out.
2) So sweat CONDENSES (turns to liquid) inside.
3) This means sweat stays inside.
4) If you sweat in a nylon coat you'll get WET.

 GORE-TEX® is breathable.

1) It lets WATER VAPOUR out.
2) This means sweat can ESCAPE.
3) So if you sweat in a GORE-TEX® coat you won't get WET.

GORE-TEX® is great for people who like doing things outdoors. They won't get wet from RAIN or from SWEAT.

Practice Questions

1) Is nylon waterproof?
2) Is nylon breathable?
3) What happens if you sweat in a coat that's not breathable?

Getting Rid of Polymers

Even though <u>plastic</u> is really useful, people are always <u>chucking it away</u>. This causes <u>problems</u>.

Non-biodegradable Plastics <u>Are Hard to Get Rid Of</u>

1) <u>BIODEGRADABLE</u> things like wood, paper and food <u>decay</u> (<u>rot</u>).
2) This means they are <u>broken down</u> by <u>bacteria</u>.
3) Most <u>polymers</u> are <u>NON-BIODEGRADABLE</u>.
4) So they <u>DON'T rot away</u>.
5) This means polymers are <u>HARD</u> to <u>get rid of</u>.

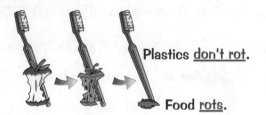

Plastics <u>don't rot</u>.

Food <u>rots</u>.

Waste Plastics <u>Cause</u> Problems...

There are <u>three ways</u> to get rid of <u>waste plastics</u>. But they all have <u>problems</u>.

WAY TO GET RID OF PLASTIC	PROBLEMS
1 <u>BURYING IN LANDFILL</u>	✗ <u>Landfill</u> sites <u>fill up</u> quickly. ✗ They're a <u>waste of land</u>. ✗ It's a <u>waste of plastic</u>.
2 <u>BURNING</u>	✗ It makes <u>poisonous gases</u>. ✗ It's a <u>waste of plastic</u>.
3 <u>RECYCLING</u>	✗ The <u>different plastics</u> all have to be <u>separated</u>. This is <u>difficult</u>.

A landfill is a hole in the ground where rubbish is put.

...So We're Trying to Make <u>Plastics That Break Down</u>

1) Scientists are making <u>POLYMERS</u> that <u>break down</u> instead of filling up <u>landfill</u>.
2) There are two sorts.

 1 <u>Polymers that BIODEGRADE</u>

2 <u>Polymers that DISSOLVE</u>

Practice Questions

1) Does <u>landfill</u> mean burying waste or burning waste?
2) What is the name for something that can be <u>broken down</u> by bacteria?
3) What are the two <u>problems</u> if you <u>burn</u> waste plastic?

Hydrocarbons — Alkanes

Hydrocarbons might sound like fancy chemicals but really they're dead easy — just hydrogen and carbon.

Hydrocarbons Are Made From Hydrogen and Carbon Atoms

1) A hydrocarbon is something that is made from <u>HYDROGEN</u> and <u>CARBON</u> atoms <u>only</u>.

2) Because it's made of <u>two sorts</u> of atom, it's called a <u>COMPOUND</u>.

3) You can <u>show</u> the atoms in a hydrocarbon using <u>blobs</u>: ⬤ = hydrogen atom
   ◯ = carbon atom

4) Or, the atoms can be shown as <u>LETTERS</u>
   — H for hydrogen, and C for carbon.

5) The <u>lines</u> in between are the <u>BONDS</u>.

Alkanes Are a Type of Hydrocarbon

1) If all the carbons are joined together by <u>SINGLE covalent bonds</u>, it's an <u>ALKANE</u>.

2) That means there's <u>only ONE line</u> between each of the atoms.

ALKANE

<u>NOT</u> an <u>ALKANE</u> —
there are <u>two lines</u> here

You need to be able to <u>spot</u> whether something is an <u>alkane</u> or not.

Molecular formula	Displayed formula	A hydrocarbon? (only H and C atoms)	An alkane? (only single bonds)
CH$_4$	H–C–H	✓	✓
C$_3$H$_8$	H–C–C–C–H	✓	✓
C$_3$H$_7$OH	H–C–C–C–O–H	✗ has an O in it	✗ if it's not a hydrocarbon it can't be an alkane
C$_3$H$_6$	H–C–C=C	✓	✗ Not just single bonds. There's a double bond too.

Have a look at page 30 if you've forgotten what molecular and displayed formulas are.

Practice Questions

1) What <u>type of bonds</u> are found in alkanes?

2) Is this molecule a <u>hydrocarbon</u>?   Cl–C–H

3) Is this molecule an <u>alkane</u>? ⟹ H–C–C–C–C–H

Hydrocarbons — Alkenes

Don't confuse <u>alkenes</u> with <u>alkanes</u> — they have <u>different bonds</u> and they <u>react differently</u>.

Alkenes *Are* Hydrocarbons *With Double Bonds*

1) <u>ALKENES</u> are <u>hydrocarbons</u> too.
2) That means they are <u>only</u> made from <u>HYDROGEN</u> and <u>CARBON</u> atoms.
3) But they're <u>NOT the same</u> as <u>ALKANES</u>.
4) This is because they have <u>DOUBLE covalent bonds</u> between some of the carbon atoms.
5) <u>Double bonds</u> are shown by <u>two lines</u>.
6) <u>TWO PAIRS</u> of <u>electrons</u> are <u>shared</u> in a double bond.

= <u>hydrogen</u> atom

= <u>carbon</u> atom

You need to be able to <u>spot alkenes</u>

Molecular formula	Displayed formula	A hydrocarbon? (only H and C in it)	An alkene? (has a double bond)
C_2H_4	H C=C H (H, H)	✓	✓
C_3H_6	H-C-C=C (H H H, H H)	✓	✓
C_3H_8	H-C-C-C-H (H H H, H H H)	✓	✗ only single bonds

Bromine Water *Goes Clear If You Add Alkenes*

1) <u>Bromine water</u> is <u>bright orange</u>.
2) You can use bromine water to <u>test</u> if you've got an <u>alkene</u>.

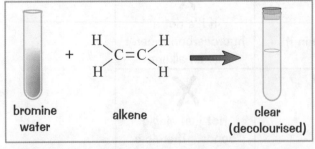

bromine water + alkene → clear (decolourised)

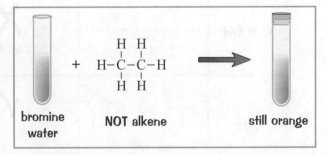

bromine water + NOT alkene → still orange

If you add an <u>ALKENE</u> to bromine water the colour will <u>change</u> from <u>orange</u> to <u>clear</u>.

<u>BUT</u> if you add something else like an <u>ALKANE</u> it <u>won't change colour</u>.

Practice Questions

1) What <u>type of atoms</u> are found in <u>alkenes</u>?
2) Is this molecule an <u>alkene</u>? ➡ H C=C-C-C-H (H H H, H H)
3) Thanos has a chemical. It turns bromine water from orange to colourless. <u>What sort of chemical</u> is it?

Fractional Distillation of Crude Oil

Fossil Fuels *Will Run Out* One Day

1) Coal, crude oil and gas are all fossil fuels.

2) They are finite resources. This means they are made VERY SLOWLY (or not made any more).

3) They're called non-renewable fuels. This is because they're being used up FASTER than they're being made.

4) So one day they'll run out.

Crude Oil *Can be Separated into Different* Fractions

CRUDE OIL

FRACTIONAL DISTILLATION

The hydrocarbons can be split into groups by FRACTIONAL DISTILLATION.

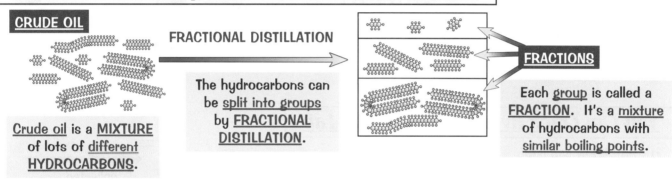

FRACTIONS

Crude oil is a MIXTURE of lots of different HYDROCARBONS.

Each group is called a FRACTION. It's a mixture of hydrocarbons with similar boiling points.

Fractional Distillation *is Done in a* Fractionating Column

Fractional distillation is done in a fractionating column:

Crude oil is HEATED.

Crude oil

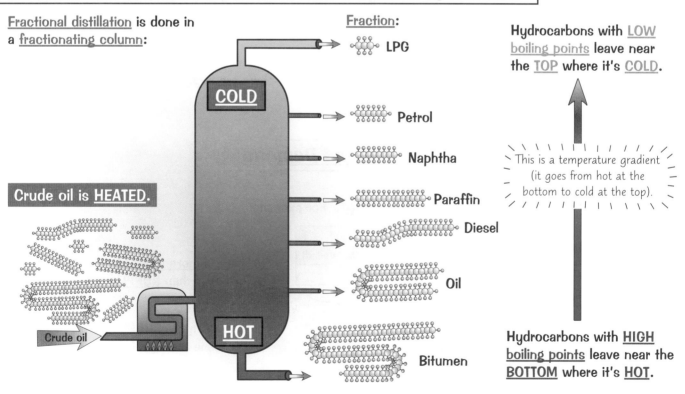

Fraction:

LPG

COLD

Petrol

Naphtha

Paraffin

Diesel

Oil

HOT

Bitumen

Hydrocarbons with LOW boiling points leave near the TOP where it's COLD.

This is a temperature gradient (it goes from hot at the bottom to cold at the top).

Hydrocarbons with HIGH boiling points leave near the BOTTOM where it's HOT.

Practice Questions

1) What does it mean when you say oil is a finite resource?

2) What is the name for a group of hydrocarbons with a similar boiling point?

3) Is the top or bottom end of a fractionating column the hottest?

Cracking

Big molecules can be split into smaller, more useful molecules. This is called cracking.

Cracking is Splitting Up Big Hydrocarbon Molecules

1) Cracking turns large alkane molecules into smaller molecules.

2) These small molecules are alkanes and alkenes.

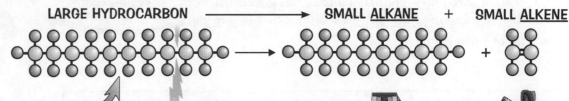

LARGE HYDROCARBON → SMALL ALKANE + SMALL ALKENE

CRACK!

3) Big hydrocarbon molecules are not very USEFUL.

4) Small hydrocarbon molecules are USEFUL. For example, PETROL is a small alkane and small alkenes are used to make POLYMERS (plastic).

You Can Crack Hydrocarbons in the Lab

1) PARAFFIN is a large hydrocarbon.

2) Here's how you CRACK paraffin in the lab:

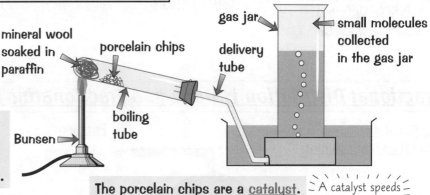

mineral wool soaked in paraffin

porcelain chips

delivery tube

gas jar

small molecules collected in the gas jar

The Bunsen heats the paraffin (cracking needs a high temperature).

Bunsen

boiling tube

The porcelain chips are a catalyst.

A catalyst speeds up a reaction.

You Need to Know About Supply and Demand

1) Supply is how much of something there IS.

2) Demand is how much of something people WANT. For example:

Fraction	Supply (approx % in crude oil)	Demand (approx % demand)
LPG	2	4
Petrol	16	27
Kerosene	13	8
Diesel	19	23
Oil and bitumen	50	38

There is more DEMAND for petrol than SUPPLY.

There is more SUPPLY of kerosene than DEMAND.

Practice Questions

1) What does cracking turn large hydrocarbons into?

2) Name two important things you need to crack paraffin in the lab.

3) What is the difference between supply and demand?

Module C1 — Carbon Chemistry

Use of Fossil Fuels

Crude oil is really useful. But it's not perfect. It can cause problems.

Oil Can Cause Big Problems

1) Accidents can happen when crude oil is moved around by ships.

2) The crude oil can get spilled in the sea and cause problems.

1 1) The oil spreads out into a big OIL SLICK.

2) Oil damages birds' FEATHERS. This can KILL them.

3) Oil also damages BEACHES.

2 1) Chemicals called detergents are used to CLEAN UP oil slicks.

2) But detergents can harm wildlife.

Some Fuels are Better than Others

There are lots of things to think about when you're deciding which is the best fuel to use:

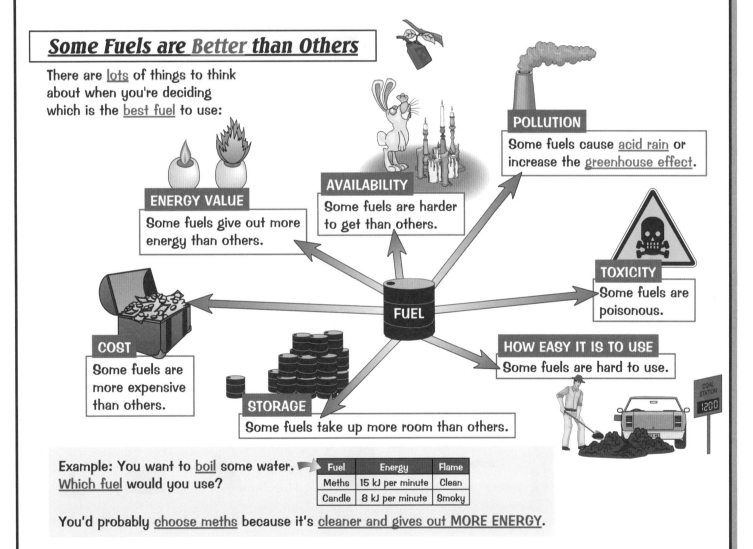

ENERGY VALUE
Some fuels give out more energy than others.

AVAILABILITY
Some fuels are harder to get than others.

POLLUTION
Some fuels cause acid rain or increase the greenhouse effect.

TOXICITY
Some fuels are poisonous.

COST
Some fuels are more expensive than others.

STORAGE
Some fuels take up more room than others.

HOW EASY IT IS TO USE
Some fuels are hard to use.

FUEL

Example: You want to boil some water. Which fuel would you use?

Fuel	Energy	Flame
Meths	15 kJ per minute	Clean
Candle	8 kJ per minute	Smoky

You'd probably choose meths because it's cleaner and gives out MORE ENERGY.

Practice Questions

1) How does oil in the sea harm birds?

2) Give four things you need to think about when choosing a fuel.

Burning Fuels

The word <u>combustion</u> crops up loads of times on this page. It may sound tricky, but it just means <u>burning</u>.

Complete Combustion Needs Oxygen

1) You need <u>OXYGEN</u> to <u>burn fuel</u>.

2) When a fuel is burned with <u>LOTS of oxygen</u> it's called <u>COMPLETE COMBUSTION</u>.

3) Complete combustion gives out <u>carbon dioxide</u>, <u>water</u>, <u>lots of HEAT</u>, and a <u>blue</u> Bunsen <u>flame</u>.

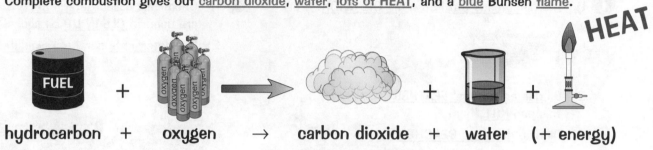

hydrocarbon + oxygen → carbon dioxide + water (+ energy)

4) You can do an <u>experiment</u> to <u>show</u> that you get <u>CARBON DIOXIDE</u> and <u>WATER</u>:

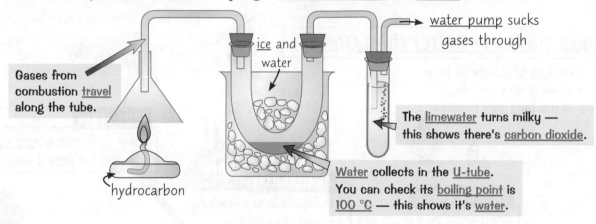

water pump sucks
gases through

Gases from combustion <u>travel</u> along the tube.

ice and water

The <u>limewater</u> turns milky — this shows there's <u>carbon dioxide</u>.

hydrocarbon

<u>Water</u> collects in the <u>U-tube</u>. You can check its <u>boiling point</u> is <u>100 °C</u> — this shows it's <u>water</u>.

With Less Oxygen You Get Incomplete Combustion

1) If you burn fuel <u>WITHOUT ENOUGH</u> oxygen you get <u>INCOMPLETE COMBUSTION</u>.

2) It makes <u>carbon monoxide</u>, <u>carbon (soot)</u>, <u>water</u>, <u>not as much HEAT</u> and a <u>yellow</u> Bunsen <u>flame</u>.

3) It's <u>not as good</u> as complete combustion because you get <u>less heat</u>, carbon monoxide is <u>POISONOUS</u>, and soot is <u>MESSY</u>.

hydrocarbon + oxygen → carbon monoxide + carbon + water (+ energy)

Practice Questions

1) What type of combustion gives a <u>blue flame</u>?

2) What type of combustion do you get if there's <u>not much oxygen</u>?

Module C1 — Carbon Chemistry

The Atmosphere

The atmosphere is all the air between the ground and space. It's made up of different gases. But it wasn't always the same as it is now.

Volcanoes Gave Out Gases that Made the Air

1) The Earth's atmosphere was made from gases that escaped from INSIDE the Earth.

2) There was lots of CARBON DIOXIDE but not much oxygen.

Plants Changed What the Air was Like

1) Plants REMOVED carbon dioxide from the air for photosynthesis.

2) Plants ADDED oxygen to the air by photosynthesis.

3) So the amount of carbon dioxide DECREASED, and the amount if oxygen INCREASED.

photosynthesis

Respiration and Burning Do The Opposite of Photosynthesis

1) Combustion (burning) and respiration (a chemical reaction done by animals) both INCREASE the amount of carbon dioxide in the air.

2) They both REDUCE the amount of oxygen in the air.

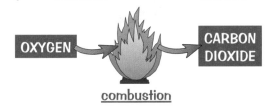

combustion

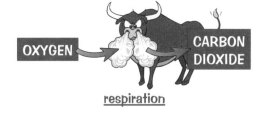

respiration

The Air Today is Mostly Nitrogen

1) Today's atmosphere has quite a lot of OXYGEN and not much CARBON DIOXIDE.

2) The amount of nitrogen, oxygen and carbon dioxide in the air today pretty much STAYS THE SAME. It's...

78% nitrogen	21% oxygen	0.035% carbon dioxide

3) There is also some water vapour in the atmosphere.

Practice Questions

1) Was oxygen a common gas in the Earth's early atmosphere?

2) Does photosynthesis add oxygen or remove oxygen from the air?

3) What are the two most common gases in the atmosphere today?

Module C1 — Carbon Chemistry

The Carbon Cycle

Carbon is everywhere. It's in the air, plants, animals, fossil fuels and the toast you had for breakfast. But it doesn't just stay in one place, it moves around between all these things in the carbon cycle...

Carbon is Always Being Recycled

The carbon on Earth moves in a big cycle:

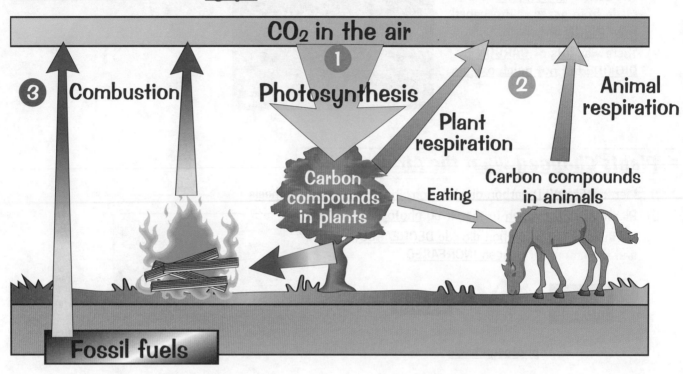

The three important things from this diagram are:

1 Photosynthesis REMOVES carbon dioxide from the air. It's done by plants.

2 Respiration ADDS carbon dioxide to the air. It's done by plants and animals.

3 Combustion (burning) ADDS carbon dioxide to the air.

Practice Questions

1) Name one way that carbon dioxide is removed from the air.
2) Name two ways that carbon dioxide is added to the air.
3) True or false: respiration is done by animals and plants.

Module C1 — Carbon Chemistry

Air Pollution and Acid Rain

When fossil fuels burn you get nasty chemicals — like <u>oxides of nitrogen</u>, <u>sulfur dioxide</u> and <u>carbon monoxide</u>. They <u>pollute</u> the air.

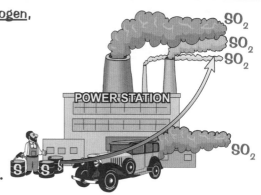

Sulfur Dioxide *Comes from Fuels*

1) <u>Fossil fuels</u> sometimes have <u>SULFUR</u> (S) in. It's an <u>impurity</u>. (An impurity is an <u>extra chemical</u> that you <u>don't want</u>.)
2) When a fuel <u>BURNS</u> the sulfur <u>burns too</u>.
3) The gas <u>SULFUR DIOXIDE</u> (SO_2) is made. This is a <u>pollutant</u>.
4) A pollutant is a <u>chemical</u> that ends up somewhere it shouldn't be.

Engines *Make* Carbon Monoxide *and* Oxides of Nitrogen

1) <u>Petrol or diesel</u> are burned in car engines.
2) If there's <u>not enough oxygen</u> then <u>INCOMPLETE</u> combustion happens.
3) This gives out <u>CARBON MONOXIDE</u>, which is a <u>poisonous gas</u>.

4) <u>OXIDES OF NITROGEN</u> are also made inside car engines.

Air Pollution *Causes* Acid Rain

<u>Acid rain</u> is nasty. It's caused by <u>sulfur dioxide</u> and <u>oxides of nitrogen</u>.

1) <u>Acid rain</u> kills <u>TREES</u>.
2) It kills <u>PLANTS</u> and <u>ANIMALS</u> in <u>lakes</u> and <u>rivers</u>.
3) It damages <u>STONE</u> buildings and <u>statues</u>, and makes <u>METALS</u> wear away (corrode).

<u>Oxides of nitrogen</u> also cause a type of air pollution called <u>photochemical smog</u>.

It's Important That *Air Pollution is Controlled*

1) <u>AIR POLLUTANTS</u> can make people <u>unhealthy</u>. For example, they might cause <u>ASTHMA</u>.
2) So air pollutants have to be <u>CONTROLLED</u>.
3) For example, <u>CATALYTIC CONVERTERS</u> stop <u>cars</u> giving out <u>carbon monoxide</u>. They change the carbon monoxide to <u>carbon dioxide</u>.

Practice Questions

1) What <u>pollutants</u> cause acid rain?
2) What <u>poisonous gas</u> might car engines give out?
3) Give two problems that <u>acid rain</u> causes.

Heat

Heating is all about <u>moving energy</u> from one place to another.

Heating Something Gives it More Energy

When something is <u>heated</u>, its particles are given <u>MORE ENERGY</u>.

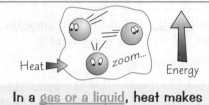

In a <u>gas or a liquid</u>, heat makes the particles <u>move around faster</u>.

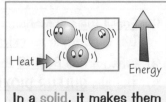

In a <u>solid</u>, it makes them <u>vibrate (shake) faster</u>.

Heat is a measure of <u>ENERGY</u>. Energy is measured in <u>JOULES (J)</u>.

High Temperature = Hot

The <u>HOTTER</u> something is, the <u>HIGHER</u> its <u>temperature</u>.

The <u>COLDER</u> something is, the <u>LOWER</u> its <u>temperature</u>.

Temperature is <u>measured</u> in <u>°C</u> (degrees Celsius).

If two things have <u>different TEMPERATURES</u>, <u>heat energy</u> will <u>FLOW</u> between them.

Room temperature is the temperature your room is at.

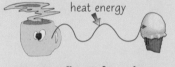

Energy flows from <u>hot objects</u> to <u>cooler</u> ones.

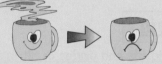

<u>HOT</u> objects <u>COOL DOWN</u> until they're at <u>room temperature</u>.

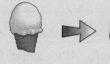

<u>COLD</u> objects <u>WARM UP</u> until they're at <u>room temperature</u>.

The <u>BIGGER</u> the <u>temperature difference</u> between a hot object and the air around it, the <u>FASTER</u> it will cool.

Thermograms Show Temperatures

1) A <u>THERMOGRAM</u> is a picture taken with a <u>camera</u> that <u>detects HEAT</u>.

2) <u>Different TEMPERATURES</u> show up as <u>different COLOURS</u>.

3) The <u>HOT</u> parts show up <u>white</u>, <u>yellow</u> and <u>red</u>.

4) The <u>COLD</u> parts show up <u>black</u>, <u>dark blue</u> and <u>purple</u>.

© TONY McCONNELL/
SCIENCE PHOTO LIBRARY

These parts of the houses are <u>hot</u>.

These parts of the houses are <u>cold</u>.

Practice Questions

1) What happens to the <u>particles</u> in a <u>gas</u> when you give them <u>more energy</u>?

2) True or false: <u>energy</u> flows from <u>hot</u> objects to <u>cooler</u> objects.

3) What do the different <u>colours</u> show on a <u>thermogram</u>?

Specific Heat Capacity

Specific heat capacity tells you how much heat energy something needs to make its temperature rise.

Specific Heat Capacity (SHC)

1) To make something's TEMPERATURE RISE, you need to give it ENERGY.

2) The AMOUNT of energy it needs depends on THREE things:

1 Its MASS (weight).

2 What it's MADE OF.

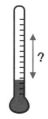

3 HOW MUCH you want the temperature to rise (the temperature change).

3) Materials that need lots of energy to warm up STORE a lot of energy.

4) HOW MUCH energy a substance can store is called its SPECIFIC HEAT CAPACITY (SHC).

> SPECIFIC HEAT CAPACITY is the amount of ENERGY needed to raise the temperature of 1 kg of a substance by 1 °C.

You Can Measure SHC

1) To find the specific heat capacity of a substance you have to measure:

- the amount of HEAT ENERGY added
- the TEMPERATURE CHANGE

2) Set up the EQUIPMENT like this:

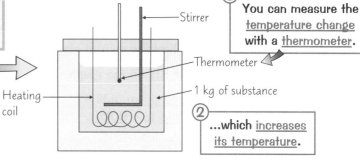

① The heating coil gives heat energy to the substance...

Stirrer

Thermometer

③ You can measure the temperature change with a thermometer.

Heating coil

1 kg of substance

② ...which increases its temperature.

Energy = Mass x SHC x Temperature Change

Look at page 6 for help with equations and formulas.

You need to be able to use this formula to calculate energy:

Energy (J)	=	Mass (kg)	×	Specific Heat Capacity (J/kg°C)	×	Temperature Change (°C)

EXAMPLE: How much energy is needed to heat 2 kg of water by 90 °C? The SHC of water is 4200 J/kg°C.

ANSWER: Energy = Mass × SHC × Temp Change = 2 kg × 4200 J/kg°C × 90 °C = 756 000 J

Practice Questions

1) What three things affect how much energy you need to increase something's temperature?

2) Work out how much energy is needed to heat 3 kg of water by 50 °C. The SHC of water is 4200 J/kg°C.

Melting and Boiling

If you want to <u>melt</u> or <u>boil</u> something you've got to give it <u>more energy</u>.

You Need Energy to Melt or Boil Something

1) This graph shows what happens to the <u>TEMPERATURE</u> of a <u>SOLID</u> when you <u>heat it up</u>:

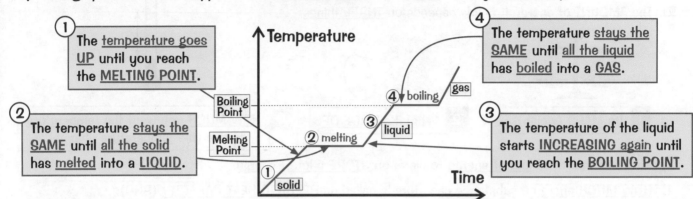

① The <u>temperature goes UP</u> until you reach the <u>MELTING POINT</u>.

② The temperature <u>stays the SAME</u> until <u>all the solid</u> has <u>melted</u> into a <u>LIQUID</u>.

④ The temperature <u>stays the SAME</u> until <u>all the liquid</u> has <u>boiled</u> into a <u>GAS</u>.

③ The temperature of the liquid starts <u>INCREASING again</u> until you reach the <u>BOILING POINT</u>.

2) The <u>FLAT BITS</u> on the graph show where a substance <u>MELTS</u> or <u>BOILS</u>.

3) <u>ALL the energy</u> you're <u>adding</u> is being used to <u>CHANGE</u> the <u>state</u>. ⬅ The <u>STATE</u> means whether it's a solid, a liquid or a gas.

4) So <u>NO energy</u> is being used to increase the temperature.

Energy is Given Out when you Freeze Something

1) When a liquid <u>FREEZES</u> (changes to a solid) it <u>GIVES OUT</u> energy.

2) When this is happening, the <u>temperature stays the SAME</u>.

3) This is shown by the <u>FLAT BIT</u> on the graph.

4) The <u>temperature doesn't go down</u> until all the substance has <u>frozen</u> to a <u>SOLID</u>.

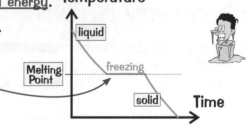

Specific Latent Heat

1) <u>SPECIFIC LATENT HEAT</u> (<u>SLH</u>) is the amount of <u>ENERGY</u> needed for <u>1 kg</u> of something to <u>CHANGE STATE</u>.

2) Specific latent heat is <u>different</u> for <u>different materials</u>.

3) Use this formula to do <u>SLH calculations</u> in the exam:

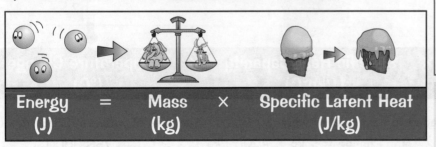

| Energy (J) | = | Mass (kg) | × | Specific Latent Heat (J/kg) |

EXAMPLE:
The SLH of ice (for melting) is 334 000 J/kg. How much energy is needed to melt an ice cube with a mass of 0.007 kg?

ANSWER:
Energy = Mass × SLH
= 0.007 kg × 334 000 J/kg
= <u>2338 J</u>

Practice Questions

1) Does the <u>temperature</u> of a substance <u>rise</u>, <u>fall</u> or <u>stay the same</u> while it's <u>melting</u>?

2) Work out how much <u>energy</u> is needed to melt a <u>5 kg</u> ice sculpture. The SLH (melting) of ice is 334 000 J/kg.

Conduction and Convection

There are <u>three</u> ways that heat can move about. <u>Conduction</u> and <u>convection</u> are up first.

In Solids Heat Flows by Conduction

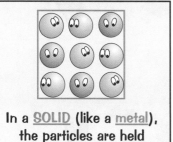

In a <u>SOLID</u> (like a <u>metal</u>), the particles are held <u>TIGHTLY together</u>.

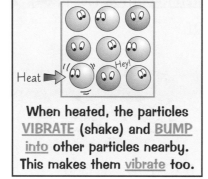

When heated, the particles <u>VIBRATE</u> (shake) and <u>BUMP into</u> other particles nearby. This makes them <u>vibrate</u> too.

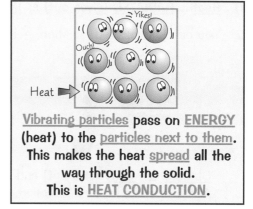

<u>Vibrating particles</u> pass on <u>ENERGY</u> (heat) to the <u>particles next to them</u>. This makes the heat <u>spread</u> all the way through the solid. This is <u>HEAT CONDUCTION</u>.

Air Is A Good Insulator

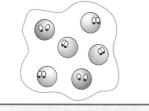

In <u>LIQUIDS and GASES</u>, the particles <u>aren't</u> held so tightly together.

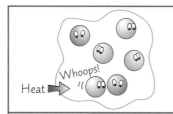

This means they don't bump into each other as much, so the heat <u>CAN'T FLOW</u> as well.

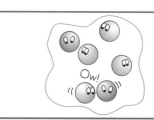

This means gases and liquids <u>DON'T CONDUCT heat</u> very well — they're good <u>INSULATORS</u>.

1) <u>AIR</u> is a <u>GOOD INSULATOR</u> because it is a <u>GAS</u>.
2) <u>TRAPPING AIR</u> inside things makes them <u>BETTER at insulating</u>.

Convection Happens in Liquids and Gases

1) <u>CONVECTION</u> is where particles with <u>more energy</u> <u>MOVE</u> from a <u>HOT</u> place to a <u>COOLER</u> one.

2) It can only happen in <u>LIQUIDS</u> and <u>GASES</u>.

3) Convection is how <u>RADIATORS</u> <u>spread warm air</u> around a room:

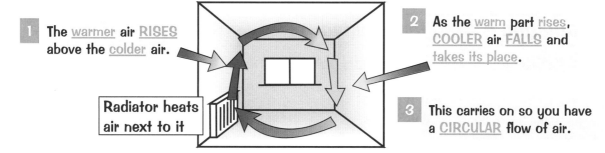

1 The <u>warmer</u> air <u>RISES</u> above the <u>colder</u> air.

2 As the <u>warm</u> part <u>rises</u>, <u>COOLER</u> air <u>FALLS</u> and <u>takes its place</u>.

3 This carries on so you have a <u>CIRCULAR</u> flow of air.

Radiator heats air next to it

4) To <u>stop convection</u>, you need to <u>STOP the liquid or gas MOVING</u>.

Practice Questions
1) True or false: in <u>solids</u>, heat flows by <u>convection</u>.
2) How can you <u>stop convection</u>?

Module P1 — Energy for the Home

Heat Radiation

Heat radiation is the third way heat can move about.

All Objects Give Out and Take in Heat Radiation

infrared radiation

1) Heat is RADIATED (given out) as INFRARED RADIATION (see p. 64).

2) You can feel infrared radiation — it's HOT.

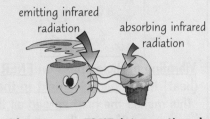

emitting infrared radiation

absorbing infrared radiation

Objects can EMIT (give out) and ABSORB (take in) heat radiation.

HOTTER objects EMIT MORE heat radiation.

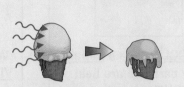

COOLER objects ABSORB heat radiation, which makes their TEMPERATURE RISE.

Colour And Texture Affect Radiation

1) MATT (dull), ROUGH and BLACK surfaces are very GOOD at absorbing and emitting heat radiation.

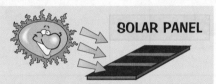

SOLAR PANEL

The panels for SOLAR WATER HEATING are painted matt black to absorb as much heat as possible.

2) WHITE or LIGHT-COLOURED, and SMOOTH surfaces are very BAD at absorbing and emitting heat radiation.

You should leave your fridge white to help keep heat away from the food inside.

3) SHINY surfaces REFLECT heat radiation — so they don't absorb it either.

The shiny surface on a PATIO HEATER REFLECTS heat downwards — onto the patio.

Heat Radiation is Used for Cooking

GRILLS and TOASTERS heat food using INFRARED RADIATION.

The heat radiated by a grill heats the surface of the food.

If you line a grill pan with SHINY FOIL, the heat is REFLECTED back onto the bottom of the food to cook it more evenly.

Practice Questions

1) True or false: heat is given out as infrared radiation.

2) Some people line grill pans with shiny foil. Explain how this helps to cook the food more evenly.

Saving Energy

It's daft to keep paying your energy bills, only to let all that energy go to waste.

Insulating Your House Saves Energy and Money

1) In the home, ENERGY flows between SOURCES and SINKS:

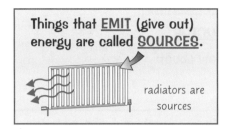

Things that EMIT (give out) energy are called SOURCES.

radiators are sources

Things that USE and WASTE or LOSE energy are called SINKS.

windows and TVs are sinks

2) There are TWO different ways you can save energy in the home:

INSULATING means doing stuff to stop heat escaping.

You can insulate your house so LESS ENERGY IS LOST through the sinks.

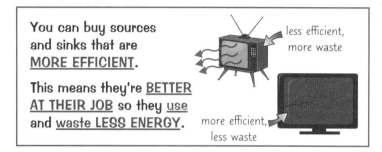

You can buy sources and sinks that are MORE EFFICIENT.

This means they're BETTER AT THEIR JOB so they use and waste LESS ENERGY.

less efficient, more waste

more efficient, less waste

3) These changes can COST A LOT at first but they make ENERGY BILLS LOWER.

Payback Time

1) After a while, the money saved on energy bills will be the SAME as the money spent on changes.

2) The time this takes is called the PAYBACK TIME.

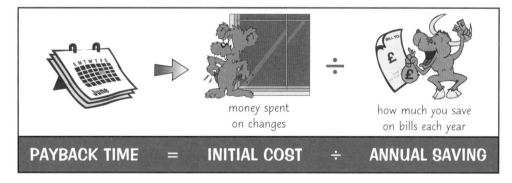

money spent on changes

how much you save on bills each year

PAYBACK TIME = INITIAL COST ÷ ANNUAL SAVING

3) The SHORTER the payback time, the BETTER VALUE FOR MONEY something is.

Practice Questions

1) True or false: sources are things that emit energy.
2) What two ways can you save energy in the home?
3) If the initial cost of double glazing is £3000 and the annual saving is £100, work out the payback time.

Saving Energy

You need to be able to explain <u>why</u> all these different types of insulation <u>save energy</u>.

There are Lots of Ways to Insulate the Home

1) To stop <u>heat energy</u> being lost, you need to <u>REDUCE CONDUCTION</u>, <u>CONVECTION</u> and <u>RADIATION</u>.

2) <u>Conduction</u> and <u>convection</u> can usually be reduced by <u>TRAPPING AIR</u>.

3) This is because <u>air</u> is a <u>GOOD INSULATOR</u> and <u>POOR CONDUCTOR</u>.

4) Here are some examples of <u>home insulation</u> you need to know about:

There's more on insulators and conductors on page 53.

LOFT INSULATION
- <u>FIBREGLASS</u>, <u>MINERAL WOOL</u> or <u>ROCK WOOL</u> are good <u>insulating materials</u>.
- When they're laid across the loft floor they <u>stop CONDUCTION</u> through the ceiling.
- This is because they're <u>poor conductors</u>.
- They also <u>trap air</u> which is a <u>good insulator</u>.

Initial Cost: £200 Annual Saving: £100
Payback time: 200 ÷ 100 = <u>2 years</u>

Check out page 55 for more on payback time.

SHINY FOIL
- Putting <u>shiny foil</u> behind wall heaters can reduce heat loss by <u>RADIATION</u>.
- The <u>heat</u> is <u>REFLECTED</u> back into the room.

THICK CURTAINS
- Thick curtains <u>reduce</u> the amount of <u>RADIATION</u> passing through the windows.
- They also <u>TRAP AIR</u> between them and the window which <u>reduces CONDUCTION</u>.

DRAUGHT-PROOFING
- Strips of foam and plastic around doors and windows <u>stop hot air going out</u>.
- This reduces <u>CONVECTION</u>.

CAVITY WALLS AND INSULATION
- Cavity walls have two layers of bricks with a <u>gap</u> between them.
- This gap reduces <u>CONDUCTION</u>.
- <u>INSULATING FOAM</u> or <u>FIBREGLASS</u> is added into the gap between layers.
- This traps pockets of <u>air</u> to reduce <u>CONVECTION</u>.

DOUBLE GLAZING
- Double glazed windows have two layers of glass with an <u>air gap</u> between them.
- This reduces <u>CONDUCTION</u>.

Practice Questions
1) Name <u>one</u> material you could use for <u>loft insulation</u>.
2) How does putting <u>shiny foil</u> behind a radiator <u>reduce heat loss</u>?
3) How does <u>draught-proofing</u> work?

Efficiency

As well as insulating your home, you can save energy by using efficient appliances.

Some Energy is Always Wasted

1) An APPLIANCE is something that uses electricity.

2) When appliances use electricity, NO ENERGY IS LOST.

3) It's just CHANGED into a different form:

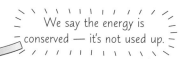
We say the energy is conserved — it's not used up.

EXAMPLE:

A TV converts electrical energy to LIGHT, SOUND and HEAT energy.

ELECTRICITY (electrical energy)

LIGHT and SOUND
This is USEFUL energy (the type of energy we want).

HEAT
This is WASTED energy.

4) For an appliance, you might only know the TOTAL energy and the amount of WASTED energy...

5) ... but you can use this equation to work out the USEFUL energy:

USEFUL energy = TOTAL energy − WASTED energy

The total energy is all the energy you've put in.

Efficient Appliances Waste Less Energy

1) EFFICIENT appliances change MOST of the energy put in to USEFUL energy.

2) This means they DON'T WASTE MUCH ENERGY.

3) You can use this equation to find efficiency:

$$\text{EFFICIENCY} = \frac{\text{USEFUL ENERGY}}{\text{TOTAL ENERGY}}$$

EXAMPLE: A light bulb uses 20 000 J of energy. 1000 J is given off as useful light energy. What is the efficiency of the bulb?

ANSWER: $\text{EFFICIENCY} = \frac{\text{USEFUL energy}}{\text{TOTAL energy}} = \frac{1000}{20\,000} = \underline{0.05}$

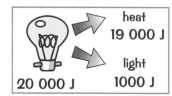
heat 19 000 J
light 1000 J
20 000 J

You Can Give Efficiency as a Percentage

You can use this equation to give the efficiency as a percentage:

$$\text{EFFICIENCY} = \frac{\text{USEFUL ENERGY}}{\text{TOTAL ENERGY}} \times 100$$

This is the same equation as before just with an extra × 100 on the end.

So, for the example above, the efficiency as a percentage would be:

$\text{EFFICIENCY} = \frac{\text{USEFUL energy}}{\text{TOTAL energy}} \times 100 = \frac{1000}{20\,000} \times 100 = \underline{5\,\%}$

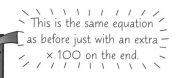
This light bulb isn't very efficient.

Practice Questions

1) True or false: efficient appliances waste most of their energy.

2) A robot is used to tickle a mouse. 300 000 J are used to tickle the mouse but 30 000 J are wasted as heat.
a) Work out the amount of useful energy. b) How efficient is the robot? Give your answer as a percentage.

Sankey Diagrams

Sankey diagrams are just a fancy way of showing <u>where energy goes</u>. Phew.

Sankey Diagrams <u>Show</u> Where Energy Goes

<u>SANKEY DIAGRAMS</u> show how much <u>energy</u> that goes <u>INTO</u> an appliance is turned into <u>USEFUL</u> energy and how much is <u>WASTED</u> energy.

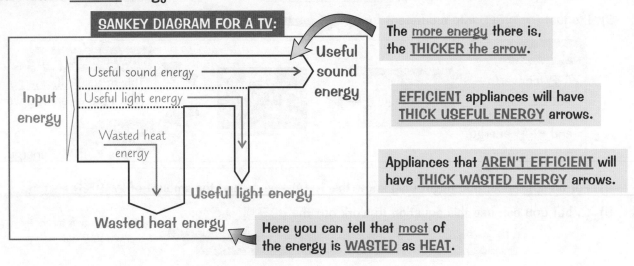

SANKEY DIAGRAM FOR A TV:

Input energy

Useful sound energy

Useful light energy

Wasted heat energy

Useful light energy

Wasted heat energy

Useful sound energy

The <u>more energy</u> there is, the <u>THICKER the arrow</u>.

<u>EFFICIENT</u> appliances will have <u>THICK USEFUL ENERGY</u> arrows.

Appliances that <u>AREN'T EFFICIENT</u> will have <u>THICK WASTED ENERGY</u> arrows.

Here you can tell that <u>most</u> of the energy is <u>WASTED</u> as <u>HEAT</u>.

Some Sankey Diagrams <u>Give You</u> More Information

1) Some Sankey diagrams can give you <u>MORE INFORMATION</u>.

2) They can tell you <u>HOW MUCH ENERGY</u> goes <u>IN</u>, is <u>WASTED</u>, and is <u>USEFUL</u>:

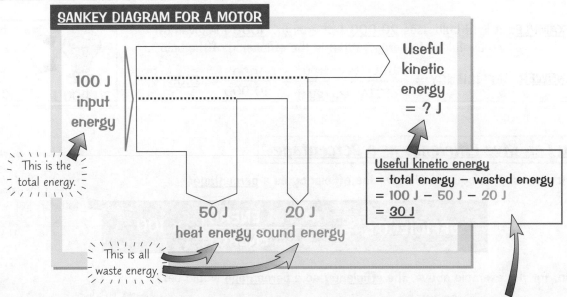

SANKEY DIAGRAM FOR A MOTOR

100 J input energy

This is the total energy.

50 J heat energy

20 J sound energy

This is all waste energy.

Useful kinetic energy = ? J

Useful kinetic energy
= total energy − wasted energy
= 100 J − 50 J − 20 J
= <u>30 J</u>

3) The useful energy is just the <u>INPUT</u> (total) energy arrow minus the <u>WASTED</u> energy arrows.

4) You can use the equation from the last page to find the <u>EFFICIENCY</u>.

Practice Questions

1) What does a <u>Sankey diagram</u> show?

2) True or false: appliances that <u>aren't efficient</u> have <u>thick</u> useful energy arrows.

Wave Basics

You have to know what all the words to do with <u>waves</u> mean, and do a little bit of maths too.

Waves **Have** Frequency, Amplitude, and Wavelength

FREQUENCY

1) This is <u>how many complete waves</u> pass a point <u>every second</u>.
2) Frequency is measured in <u>hertz (Hz)</u> — 1 Hz is <u>1 wave per second</u>.

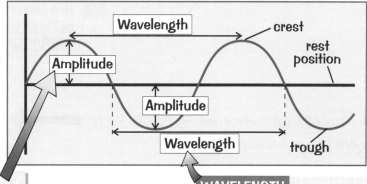

AMPLITUDE

This is the distance from the <u>rest position</u> to a <u>crest</u> or <u>trough</u>.

WAVELENGTH

1) This is the length of a <u>full cycle</u> of the wave.
2) For example, measuring the distance from <u>crest to crest</u> gives you the <u>wavelength</u>.

Wave Speed **=** Frequency **x** Wavelength

This equation lets you work out the <u>SPEED OF A WAVE</u>:

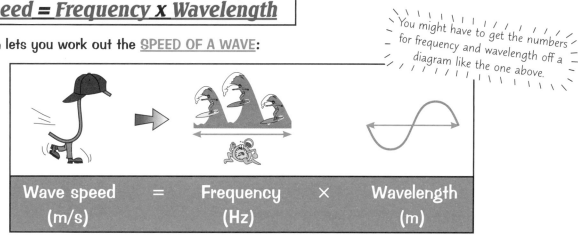

You might have to get the numbers for frequency and wavelength off a diagram like the one above.

Wave speed (m/s)	=	Frequency (Hz)	×	Wavelength (m)

EXAMPLE:
Calculate the speed of a wave with frequency 0.5 Hz and wavelength 0.9 m.

ANSWER:
Wave speed = frequency × wavelength
= 0.5 Hz × 0.9 m
= <u>0.45 m/s</u>

All <u>ELECTROMAGNETIC WAVES</u> (see p. 62) travel at the <u>same high SPEED</u> in a vacuum.

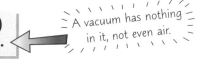

A vacuum has nothing in it, not even air.

Practice Questions

1) What is the <u>amplitude</u> of a <u>wave</u>?
2) Calculate the <u>speed</u> of a wave with frequency <u>3 Hz</u> and wavelength <u>0.5 m</u>.

Wave Properties — Reflection

Now you know the basics, let's have a look at some wave properties.

All Waves Can be Reflected, Diffracted and Refracted

 An obstacle is anything that gets in the way.

1 All ELECTROMAGNETIC WAVES (see p. 62) travel in a straight line.

electromagnetic wave

glass block

2 When waves meet an obstacle or new substance, they may CHANGE DIRECTION.

3 This can happen by REFLECTION, DIFFRACTION or REFRACTION.

Reflection

1) A PLANE SURFACE is a smooth, flat surface that REFLECTS WELL. 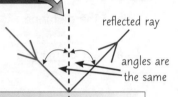 A mirror is a plane surface.

2) REFLECTING LIGHT RAYS always follow this RULE:

ANGLE OF THE RAY HITTING THE SURFACE = ANGLE OF THE RAY BOUNCING OFF

3) Use this rule to draw RAY DIAGRAMS.

reflected ray
angles are the same

Drawing Ray Diagrams

1. DRAW THE NORMAL

Draw a dotted line at right angles to the surface, at the point where the ray meets the surface. This line is called the NORMAL.

Normal
Surface

2. FIND THE ANGLE OF THE RAY HITTING THE SURFACE

Measure the ANGLE between the ray and the normal.

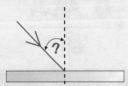

3. DRAW THE ANGLE OF THE RAY BOUNCING OFF

Angle of the ray hitting the surface = angle of the ray bouncing off.

So draw in the reflected ray at the SAME ANGLE but on the OTHER SIDE of the normal.

draw the ray so these angles are the same

- You might have to draw a diagram showing MORE THAN ONE reflection.
- Just take your time and follow the steps above for EACH REFLECTION.

Practice Questions

1) True or false: electromagnetic waves travel in a straight line.
2) Complete this rule for drawing ray diagrams: angle of the ray hitting the surface = ?

Module P1 — Energy for the Home

Diffraction and Refraction

If you liked reflection, you'll love diffraction and refraction — they're awesome.

Diffraction

1) All waves SPREAD OUT at the edges when they pass through a GAP or PASS AN OBJECT.

2) This is called DIFFRACTION:

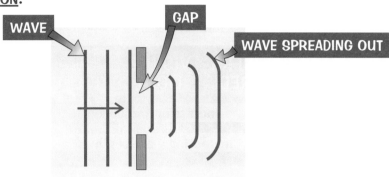

Refraction

1) Waves travel at DIFFERENT SPEEDS in DIFFERENT SUBSTANCES:

2) So, when a wave passes from one substance to another it CHANGES SPEED.

3) This change in speed can make the wave CHANGE DIRECTION.

4) This is called REFRACTION:

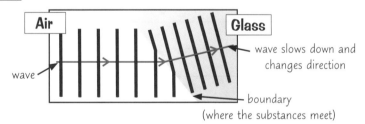

5) Waves are ONLY refracted if they meet the boundary AT AN ANGLE.

6) If they're travelling at right angles to the boundary they will change speed, but NOT direction:

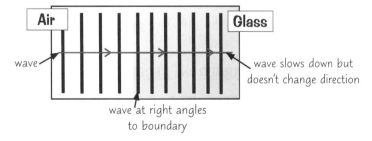

Practice Questions

1) True or false: diffraction is when waves spread out as they pass through a gap or pass an object.

2) What is refraction?

EM Waves and Communication

There is <u>no end</u> to the things you can do with a wave — especially <u>electromagnetic waves</u>.

The Electromagnetic Spectrum

1) There are <u>SEVEN</u> different types of <u>ELECTROMAGNETIC (EM) WAVES</u>.

2) They all have <u>DIFFERENT WAVELENGTHS</u> and <u>FREQUENCIES</u>.

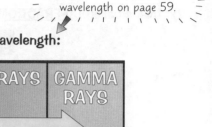
There's more on frequency and wavelength on page 59.

3) You need to know their <u>names</u> and <u>list them in order</u> by frequency and wavelength:

RADIO WAVES	MICRO WAVES	INFRA RED	VISIBLE LIGHT	ULTRA VIOLET	X-RAYS	GAMMA RAYS

Increasing frequency →

← Increasing wavelength

These waves have low frequencies and long wavelengths.

These waves have high frequencies and short wavelengths.

Some EM Waves Are Used To Send Information

1) EM waves are used in <u>communications</u> to <u>SEND INFORMATION</u>.

2) You need to learn these <u>uses</u>:

EM WAVE	HOW IT'S USED
VISIBLE LIGHT	optical fibres (see p. 65)
INFRARED	TV remote controls optical fibres 'night vision' cameras
MICROWAVES	mobile phones satellite communications
RADIO WAVES	radar TV and radio

The Size of a Receiver Depends on the Size of the Wave

1) We use <u>different RECEIVERS</u> to <u>pick up</u> the different types of <u>EM waves</u> used for communication.

2) The <u>LONGER</u> the <u>WAVELENGTH</u>, the <u>LARGER</u> the <u>RECEIVER</u> should be.

3) So <u>RADIO WAVES</u> need the <u>BIGGEST RECEIVERS</u>.

EXAMPLE

<u>Satellite dishes</u> are used to pick up <u>microwaves</u>.

Practice Questions

1) Which EM waves have a <u>higher frequency</u>, microwaves or infrared?

2) Name <u>one</u> type of wave used in <u>optical fibres</u>.

3) Which EM waves need a <u>larger receiver</u>, infrared or microwaves?

Communicating with Light and Lasers

Light is used for <u>communicating</u>.

Sending Messages with Light Needs a Code

1) In the past, light was used to <u>SPEED UP</u> communication.

2) It was also used to send messages over <u>LONG DISTANCES</u>.

3) Messages could be sent by <u>flashing a light ON and OFF</u> in a <u>CODE</u>.

4) <u>MORSE CODE</u> was used a lot.

MORSE CODE

a = • —

b = — • • •

c = — • — •

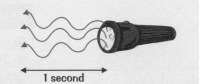

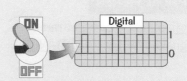

Each <u>letter</u> and each <u>number</u> is given a pattern of '<u>DOTS</u>' and '<u>DASHES</u>'.

These are <u>PULSES</u> of light (or <u>sound</u>) made by switching the light source <u>on</u> and <u>off</u>.

Morse code is a <u>DIGITAL SIGNAL</u> (see p. 68) because the light pulse is only '<u>on</u>' or '<u>off</u>'.

Lasers are Made of Light

1) A <u>LASER</u> is just a <u>special ray of light</u>.

2) All the <u>light</u> in a laser is a <u>SINGLE COLOUR</u>.

3) Light that's all <u>one colour</u> is called <u>MONOCHROMATIC LIGHT</u>.

4) Lasers are <u>THIN</u> and <u>STRONG</u>.

5) This means they can be <u>used</u> for lots of things:

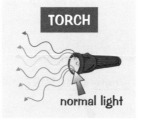

TORCH

normal light

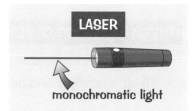

LASER

monochromatic light

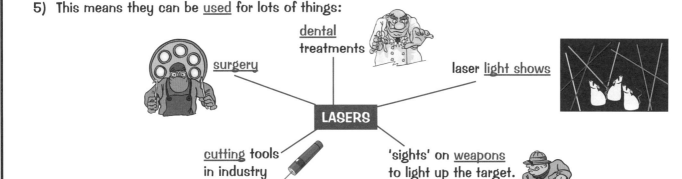

dental treatments

surgery

laser <u>light shows</u>

LASERS

<u>cutting</u> tools in industry

'sights' on <u>weapons</u> to light up the target.

Practice Questions

1) What <u>code</u> was used a lot in the past to send <u>messages</u> using <u>light</u>?

2) True or false: <u>monochromatic</u> light is made up of <u>lots of colours</u>.

3) Give <u>one use</u> of <u>lasers</u>.

Infrared

Infrared is also useful for <u>communicating</u>.

Infrared Has Many Uses

<u>Infrared radiation</u> (IR) can be used for:

SENDING INFORMATION SHORT DISTANCES

- IR can be used to <u>send information</u> between <u>mobile phones</u> or <u>computers</u>.
- But it only works over <u>SHORT DISTANCES</u>.

OPTICAL FIBRES

<u>Optical fibres</u> carry infrared signals over <u>LONG DISTANCES</u>.

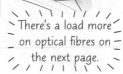

There's a load more on optical fibres on the next page.

REMOTE CONTROLS

<u>Remote controls</u> send information to <u>TVs</u> and <u>video</u> and <u>DVD</u> players using <u>IR</u> (see below).

SECURITY SYSTEMS

- <u>IR sensors</u> can 'see' <u>BODY HEAT</u>.
- So they are used in things like <u>burglar alarms</u>.
- When a person <u>walks in front</u> of the sensor, it 'sees' their body heat and <u>turns on</u> an <u>ALARM</u>.

THERMAL IMAGING CAMERAS

- <u>Thermal imaging cameras</u> work like IR sensors.
- They 'see' <u>HEAT</u> and use it to <u>create</u> a <u>PICTURE</u>.

There's an example of one of these pictures on page 50.

AUTOMATIC DOORS

<u>Automatic doors</u> have <u>IR sensors</u> on them.

IR Signals Can Control Electrical Equipment

1) <u>REMOTE CONTROLS</u> can control <u>electronic equipment</u>.
2) They work by <u>FLASHING infrared light</u> in different <u>PATTERNS</u>.
3) The pattern acts as a <u>CODE</u>.
4) This <u>code</u> tells the electronic equipment <u>WHAT TO DO</u>.

CODE

play = • — • •

pattern of flashes

Practice Questions

1) Give <u>two uses</u> for <u>infrared radiation</u>.
2) Explain how a <u>remote control</u> works.

Optical Fibres

Optical fibres work by total internal reflection.

Total Internal Reflection Depends on the Critical Angle

1) When a ray of light meets a BOUNDARY it might go through or bounce back. ➡

2) What happens depends on the SUBSTANCE on each side of the boundary.

3) Every substance has its own, different CRITICAL ANGLE.

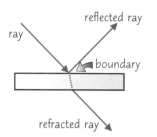

If the ANGLE a ray hits the boundary at is BIGGER THAN THE CRITICAL ANGLE, you get TOTAL INTERNAL REFLECTION.

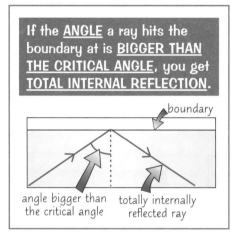

angle bigger than the critical angle | totally internally reflected ray

If the angle is the SAME AS the critical angle, most of the ray goes ALONG THE SURFACE, and some is REFLECTED.

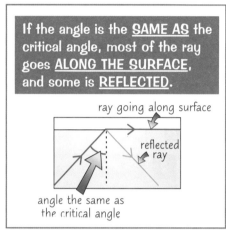

angle the same as the critical angle

If the angle is SMALLER than the critical angle, some of the ray is REFLECTED, but most is REFRACTED.

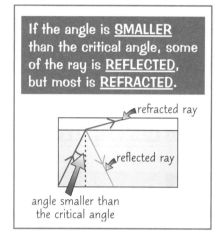

angle smaller than the critical angle

4) Total internal reflection can happen at a boundary between AIR and:

- GLASS,
- WATER,
- PERSPEX (see-through plastic).

Light and Infrared Can Travel Through Optical Fibres

1) OPTICAL FIBRES can carry DATA (information) really quickly over long distances.

2) They carry the data as pulses of visible light or infrared rays.

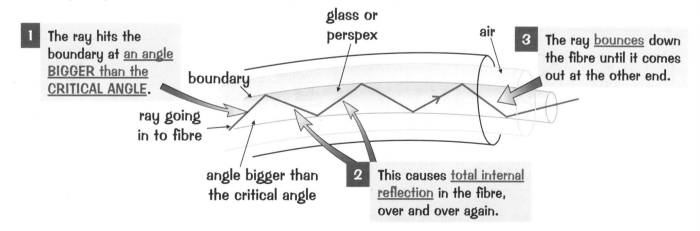

1 The ray hits the boundary at an angle BIGGER than the CRITICAL ANGLE.

ray going in to fibre

boundary

glass or perspex

air

3 The ray bounces down the fibre until it comes out at the other end.

angle bigger than the critical angle

2 This causes total internal reflection in the fibre, over and over again.

Practice Questions

1) True or false: if a ray hits a boundary at an angle smaller than the critical angle, you get total internal reflection.
2) Do optical fibres carry data as pulses of visible light or pulses of sound waves?

Microwaves

Microwaves have two main uses — <u>communication</u> and <u>cooking food</u>.

Microwaves Carry Mobile Phone Signals

1) Mobile phones use <u>MICROWAVE SIGNALS</u>.

2) Microwaves <u>DON'T DIFFRACT</u> (bend or spread out) much. (See page 61.)

3) This means that mobile phone <u>MASTS</u> need to be in <u>line of sight</u> of each other.

4) If there's an <u>obstacle</u> like a hill in the way, you might get a <u>POOR SIGNAL</u>.

line of sight

no obstacles in the way

Microwaves are also affected by <u>WATER</u>.

So in <u>wet weather</u>, or if you're near a <u>lake</u>, you can get a <u>poor signal</u> too.

Microwave Ovens Cook Food

1

1 cm

cold pie

In a <u>microwave oven</u>, microwaves <u>PENETRATE</u> (enter) about <u>1 cm</u> into <u>FOOD</u>.

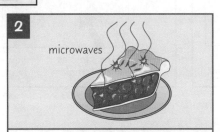

2

microwaves

The <u>microwaves</u> are <u>ABSORBED</u> (taken in) by <u>WATER</u> or <u>FAT</u> molecules in the food.

3

hot pie

This <u>HEATS</u> the food up.

1) Microwaves can <u>pass through GLASS</u> and <u>PLASTICS</u>.

2) But microwave ovens have a <u>shiny metal case</u> to <u>REFLECT</u> the microwaves.

3) This <u>stops</u> the <u>microwaves</u> getting <u>OUT</u>.

4) Microwaves can cause <u>BURNS</u> if they are <u>absorbed</u> by your <u>body tissue</u>.

Mobile Phone Microwaves May be Dangerous

Some people think that microwaves from <u>mobile phones</u> and <u>masts</u> might be <u>DANGEROUS</u>.

People who <u>use mobile phones</u> or <u>live near masts</u> might be at <u>risk</u>.

You'd be <u>MORE at risk</u> the <u>MORE</u> you <u>use your phone</u>.

There's <u>no real PROOF</u> that mobile phones are dangerous though.

- <u>Different studies</u> have found <u>CONFLICTING</u> (<u>opposite</u>) results so scientists <u>CAN'T AGREE</u> with each other.

- The results of studies are <u>PUBLISHED</u> so they can be <u>checked</u> by other scientists until <u>everyone agrees</u>.

Practice Questions

1) Name <u>one</u> thing that could give you a <u>poor mobile phone signal</u>.

2) True or false: microwaves can pass though <u>glass</u> and <u>plastic</u>.

Wireless Communication

Shouting is a good way to <u>communicate without wires</u>. But <u>radio waves</u> are probably a better option.

Wireless Technology *Doesn't Use Wires*

1) <u>WIRELESS TECHNOLOGY</u> uses <u>electromagnetic radiation</u> (p. 62).

2) It's used for <u>communication WITHOUT WIRES</u>, in things like:

 mobile phones
 radios
 TVs
 laptop computers

ADVANTAGES (GOOD POINTS)	DISADVANTAGE (BAD POINT)

- It's <u>CONVENIENT</u> (makes life easier).
- There's <u>NO NEED</u> for <u>wires</u> or a connection to a <u>telephone line</u>.
- It's <u>PORTABLE</u> (you can use it <u>on the move</u>).

You <u>need an aerial</u> to pick up the signals.

All Waves *Can be Reflected* and *Refracted*

1) When waves meet an <u>object</u> or <u>new substance</u>, they could be:

- <u>REFLECTED</u> — they bounce off the obstacle or substance.
- <u>REFRACTED</u> — they <u>change direction</u>.

electromagnetic wave   reflection   refraction

2) This can be a <u>GOOD THING</u> for communication:

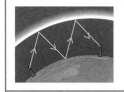 Radio waves can travel <u>much</u> **FURTHER** using **REFLECTION**.

3) It can also be a <u>BAD THING</u>:

obstacle   refracted signal

REFRACTION can <u>bend signals</u>, so the signal is <u>LOST</u>.

Radio Waves *Can Interfere with* Each Other

1) <u>Radio stations</u> send out <u>radio waves</u> of a certain <u>FREQUENCY</u>.

2) Radio stations <u>near</u> to each other often use <u>DIFFERENT frequencies</u>.

3) This is so the signals don't <u>INTERFERE</u> (get mixed up) as much.

4) <u>Digital Audio Broadcasting</u> (DAB) is different to normal <u>FM</u> radio:

Frequency is covered on page 59.   different frequencies

ADVANTAGES OF DAB	• There's <u>less interference</u> with other radio stations. • There are <u>more radio stations</u> available.

DISADVANTAGES OF DAB	• Some areas <u>can't pick up DAB</u> at the moment. • The <u>sound quality</u> of DAB is often <u>not as good</u> as an <u>FM</u> radio broadcast.

Practice Questions

1) Give <u>one use</u> of <u>wireless technology</u>.

2) Give <u>one disadvantage</u> of using <u>DAB</u> instead of FM radio.

Analogue and Digital Signals

Information is sent as a <u>signal</u>. There are <u>two</u> different types of signal.

Information is Changed into Signals

1) <u>INFORMATION</u> (like sounds or pictures for your TV) is changed into <u>SIGNALS</u> before it's sent anywhere.

2) The signals can either be <u>ANALOGUE</u> or <u>DIGITAL</u>.

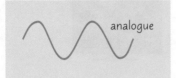
analogue

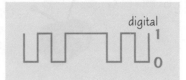
digital
1
0

Analogue Signals can have Any Number

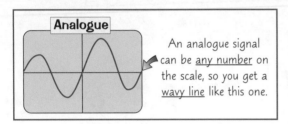

Analogue

An analogue signal can be <u>any number</u> on the scale, so you get a <u>wavy line</u> like this one.

1) An <u>analogue</u> signal can have <u>ANY NUMBER</u>.

2) Remember: <u>AN</u>alogue — <u>AN</u>y.

3) We say it can <u>vary CONTINUOUSLY</u>.

Digital Signals are Just On or Off

1) A <u>DIGITAL</u> signal can only be one of <u>TWO</u> values.

2) These values are usually <u>ON</u> (<u>1</u>) and <u>OFF</u> (<u>0</u>).

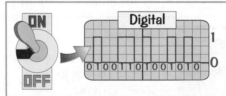

ON
OFF

Digital
1
0
0 1 0 0 1 1 0 1 0 0 1 0 1 0

A digital signal can only be <u>0 or 1</u>, so you get a <u>square-shaped</u> line like this one.

Digital Signals Can Be Better Than Analogue

1) All signals pick up <u>NOISE</u> when they travel long distances.

2) It is much <u>easier</u> to <u>REMOVE NOISE</u> from <u>digital</u> signals:

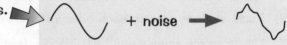
+ noise

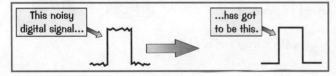

This noisy digital signal...

...has got to be this.

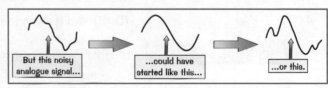

But this noisy analogue signal...

...could have started like this...

...or this.

3) This makes digital signals <u>MUCH BETTER</u> for things like <u>TV</u> and <u>radio</u>.

Practice Questions

1) What type of signal can have <u>any number</u>?

2) True or false: all signals pick up <u>silence</u> when they <u>travel long distances</u>.

3) Why are <u>digital signals</u> better for things like <u>TV</u> and <u>radio</u>?

Ultraviolet Radiation

You've seen how <u>useful</u> waves can be — but they can also be pretty <u>bad</u> for us.

Ultraviolet Radiation Can Cause Problems

There's more on <u>EM</u> radiation on page 62.

1) The <u>Sun's rays</u> contain <u>ULTRAVIOLET RADIATION</u> (UV).

2) UV can <u>DAMAGE CELLS</u>.

3) If you spend a <u>lot of time</u> in the <u>Sun</u>, you could get:

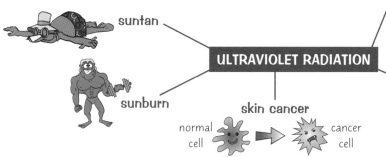

suntan

premature skin ageing
(e.g. wrinkles when
you're young :s)

ULTRAVIOLET RADIATION

sunburn

skin cancer

cataracts
(an eye condition)

normal cell → cancer cell

Darker Skin can Protect you from UV

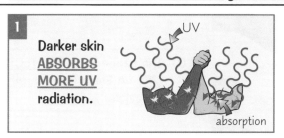

1 Darker skin <u>ABSORBS MORE UV</u> radiation.

UV

absorption

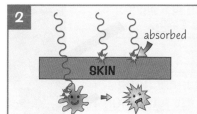

2

absorbed

SKIN

This means <u>LESS UV</u> reaches <u>body cells</u>.

So darker skin <u>REDUCES</u> the <u>risk of cancer</u>.

Sunscreens have Different Ratings

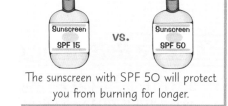

Sunscreen SPF 15   vs.   Sunscreen SPF 50

The sunscreen with SPF 50 will protect you from burning for longer.

1) <u>SUNSCREENS</u> (sun block or sun cream) <u>PROTECT</u> us from <u>UV</u>.

2) They all have a <u>SUN PROTECTION FACTOR</u> (SPF).

3) The <u>HIGHER</u> the SPF, the <u>LESS DAMAGE</u> done.

4) This means the <u>higher</u> the SPF, the <u>LONGER</u> you can stay in the sun <u>WITHOUT BURNING</u>.

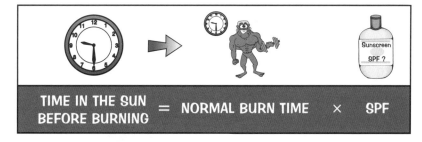

Sunscreen SPF ?

TIME IN THE SUN BEFORE BURNING = NORMAL BURN TIME × SPF

<u>EXAMPLE</u>: Ruvani normally burns after <u>40 minutes</u> in the sun. She applies sunscreen with <u>SPF 8</u>. For how long can she sunbathe before she will start to burn?

<u>ANSWER</u>: Time before burning = normal burn time × SPF
= 40 mins × 8 = 320 minutes = <u>5 hours and 20 minutes</u>.

Practice Questions

1) Other than a suntan, name <u>two things</u> that you could get if you spend a long time in the <u>Sun</u>.

2) True or false: the <u>higher</u> the <u>SPF</u>, the <u>longer</u> you can stay in the <u>Sun</u> <u>without burning</u>.

UV and the Ozone Layer

Scientists try and protect us from UV.

We Know the Risks of UV

Scientists and the government tell us about the RISKS OF UV through the NEWS and ADVERTISING.

They tell us this so we know how to KEEP SAFE, which helps to improve everyone's HEALTH.

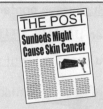

We're also warned of the risks of using SUNBEDS. They can cause the same damage as too much sun.

The Ozone Layer Protects Us

1) The OZONE LAYER is a layer of gas around the Earth.

2) It ABSORBS UV RADIATION from the Sun.

3) The ozone layer PROTECTS LIFE on Earth from harmful ultraviolet radiation.

There's a Hole in the Ozone Layer

1) Scientists found that the AMOUNT of ozone over ANTARCTICA was DROPPING.

2) This fall in the amount of ozone was UNEXPECTED.

3) The low level of ozone looks like a 'hole'.

4) Scientists came up with an EXPLANATION for it — then did lots of TESTS to see if they were right.

5) DIFFERENT SCIENTISTS carried out tests too, using lots of DIFFERENT EQUIPMENT.

hole in the ozone layer

harmful UV rays can reach the Earth.

Practice Questions

1) How does the government tell us about the risks of UV?

2) What is the ozone layer?

3) True or false: the fall in the amount of ozone was expected.

Seismic Waves

Earthquakes make <u>different</u> types of <u>waves</u>.

Earthquakes Cause Waves

1) <u>Earthquakes</u> cause waves called <u>SEISMIC WAVES</u> (shock waves):

2) Seismic waves can <u>cause</u>:

DAMAGE TO THE EARTH'S SURFACE

DAMAGE TO BUILDINGS

TIDAL WAVES (TSUNAMIS)

There are waves on the <u>surface</u>...

...and waves <u>inside the Earth</u>.

3) Seismic waves are <u>detected</u> (picked up) by <u>SEISMOMETERS</u> and recorded on <u>SEISMOGRAPHS</u>.

Seismometers <u>measure</u> how much the <u>ground wobbles</u>.
Seismographs <u>show</u> how much the ground wobbles on a <u>graph</u>.

P- and S-Waves are Seismic Waves

<u>P-WAVES</u> and <u>S-WAVES</u> are two types of <u>seismic wave</u>:

P-Waves are Longitudinal

1) <u>P-WAVES</u> travel through <u>SOLIDS</u> and <u>LIQUIDS</u>.

2) They travel <u>FASTER</u> than <u>S-waves</u>.

3) They're <u>LONGITUDINAL</u> waves:

LONGITUDINAL WAVES (like a slinky spring pushed in and out)

Vibrations along the same direction as wave is travelling

S-Waves are Transverse

1) <u>S-WAVES</u> only travel through <u>SOLIDS</u>.

2) They're <u>SLOWER</u> than <u>P-waves</u>.

3) They're <u>TRANSVERSE</u> waves:

TRANSVERSE WAVES (like a slinky spring wiggled from side to side)

Vibrations from side to side

Wave travelling this way

Practice Questions

1) Name <u>two</u> types of <u>seismic waves</u>.

2) Which of the waves in practice question 1) are <u>longitudinal</u> waves?

Classification

Classification is when you <u>sort things</u> into <u>groups</u>. Biologists sort <u>living things</u> into groups all the time...

Classification **Puts** Living Organisms **into** Groups

1) Living organisms can be sorted into <u>GROUPS</u>.
2) Members of the <u>same group</u> have the <u>same CHARACTERISTICS</u> (features).
3) The <u>biggest</u> groups are called <u>kingdoms</u>. Kingdoms are <u>SPLIT UP</u> into <u>smaller</u> and <u>smaller groups</u>:

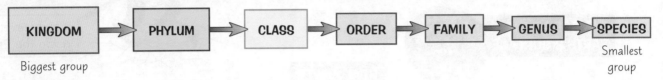

KINGDOM → PHYLUM → CLASS → ORDER → FAMILY → GENUS → SPECIES

Biggest group   Smallest group

An organism is a creature.

Classification **Can be** Tricky

1) It can be <u>hard</u> to put organisms into <u>groups</u>. That's because <u>some organisms</u> fit into <u>more than one group</u>.

2) But classification is <u>important</u>. It <u>helps</u> us to <u>understand</u>:

ECOLOGICAL RELATIONSHIPS between organisms.

For example, how organisms that live in the same place affect each other.

EVOLUTIONARY RELATIONSHIPS between organisms (how they're related).

For example, dogs are related to wolves.

There are Five Kingdoms

You need to know the <u>characteristics</u> of <u>organisms</u> in each of the <u>five kingdoms</u>:

Organisms in the <u>PLANT KINGDOM</u>...	Organisms in the <u>ANIMAL KINGDOM</u>...	Organisms in the <u>FUNGI KINGDOM</u>...	Organisms in the <u>PROTOCTISTA</u> <u>KINGDOM</u>...	Organisms in the <u>PROKARYOTE</u> <u>KINGDOM</u>...
1) Are <u>multicellular</u> (they have lots of cells). 2) Have <u>cell walls</u>.	1) Are <u>multicellular</u>. 2) <u>Don't</u> have <u>cell walls</u>.	1) Are <u>multicellular</u>. 2) Have <u>cell walls</u>.	Are <u>single-celled</u> organisms (they only have one cell).	Are <u>single-celled</u> organisms.
Use <u>energy</u> from the <u>sun</u> to make their own <u>food</u>. They do this using <u>photosynthesis</u>.	<u>Feed</u> on <u>other organisms</u>.	<u>Reproduce</u> using <u>spores</u>.	Have a <u>nucleus</u>. This <u>controls</u> the <u>cell</u>.	<u>Don't</u> have a <u>nucleus</u>.

Practice Questions
1) Why can it be hard to put living things into <u>groups</u>?
2) Give <u>two</u> characteristics of the <u>plant kingdom</u>.

More On Classification

Yep, there's more where that came from...

There are Four Main Groups of Arthropods

1) ARTHROPODS are part of the animal kingdom.
2) They're also INVERTEBRATES. This means they DON'T HAVE a skeleton inside their body.
3) Arthropods have a hard outer shell instead.
4) There are four main groups of arthropods:

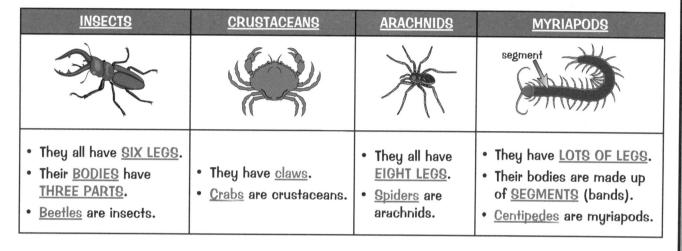

INSECTS	CRUSTACEANS	ARACHNIDS	MYRIAPODS
• They all have SIX LEGS. • Their BODIES have THREE PARTS. • Beetles are insects.	• They have claws. • Crabs are crustaceans.	• They all have EIGHT LEGS. • Spiders are arachnids.	• They have LOTS OF LEGS. • Their bodies are made up of SEGMENTS (bands). • Centipedes are myriapods.

Evolutionary Trees Show Relationships Between Species

1) EVOLUTIONARY TREES show how organisms are related. Here's an example:

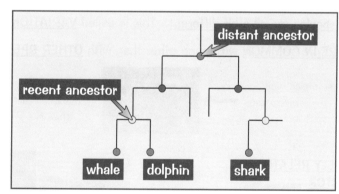

Your ancestors are the people in your family that came before you, like your parents and grandparents.

2) This evolutionary tree shows that:

- Whales and dolphins are more closely related than whales and sharks.
- This is because whales and dolphins share the same recent ancestor. Whales and sharks only share a distant ancestor.

Practice Questions

1) Give two characteristics of insects.
2) What do evolutionary trees show?

Species

If you've ever wanted to <u>name</u> your own <u>species</u>, you're in luck — this page tells you how you do it.

You Need to Know What A Species Is...

A <u>SPECIES</u> is a group of organisms which can <u>INTERBREED</u> to produce <u>FERTILE OFFSPRING</u>.

'Interbreed' means they can reproduce together.

'Offspring' is another word for children. 'Fertile' just means able to have children.

You Name Species Using The Binomial System

See page 72 for more on genus and species.

1) Scientists use the <u>BINOMIAL SYSTEM</u> to give each species a <u>name</u>.

2) Each name has <u>TWO PARTS</u>.

   • The first part is the <u>GENUS</u>.
   • The second part is the <u>SPECIES</u>.

For example, humans are called:

This bit is the genus. **Homo sapiens** This bit is the species.

3) The <u>binomial system</u> is used <u>all over the world</u>.

4) It means scientists who speak <u>different languages</u> can use the <u>same name</u> for each species.

5) This <u>STOPS</u> them getting species <u>CONFUSED</u>.

There's Variation in Every Species

1) Members of the <u>same species</u> are all <u>a bit different</u>. This is called <u>VARIATION</u>.

2) But they still have <u>MORE IN COMMON</u> with each other than with <u>OTHER SPECIES</u>.

For example, these dogs are the same species. They don't look much alike...

...but the dogs look more like each other than like a frog.

3) Species that are <u>CLOSELY RELATED</u> have a <u>RECENT ANCESTOR</u>. They usually <u>look similar</u> and live in <u>similar habitats</u>.

For example, dolphins and whales have a recent ancestor.

See page 73 for more on ancestors.

4) But <u>some</u> closely related species <u>look DIFFERENT</u>. This is because they live in <u>different habitats</u>.

Zebras and horses are closely related, but they look very different.

Practice Questions

1) What is a <u>species</u>?
2) Give one reason why two <u>closely related species</u> might look <u>different</u>.

Food Chains and Food Webs

Living things eat each other. Grim, but true. And you can show this by drawing <u>food chains</u> and <u>food webs</u>.

Food Chains Show What Eats What

1) <u>FOOD CHAINS</u> show what <u>eats</u> what. Here's an example:

Grass   is eaten by...   Mouse   is eaten by...   Owl

2) Food chains always <u>start</u> with a <u>PRODUCER</u>. These are living things that <u>make their own food</u>.

3) <u>Green plants</u> (like grass) are <u>producers</u>. So are <u>seaweeds</u>.

4) Food chains also have <u>consumers</u>:

The mouse is a <u>PRIMARY CONSUMER</u>. It <u>eats producers</u>.

The owl is a <u>SECONDARY CONSUMER</u>. It <u>eats primary consumers</u>.

5) Each stage in a food chain called a <u>TROPHIC LEVEL</u>. For example, <u>grass</u> is the <u>first</u> trophic level. The <u>mouse</u> is the <u>second</u> trophic level. And the <u>owl</u> is the <u>third</u> trophic level.

Food Webs are Made from Lots of Food Chains

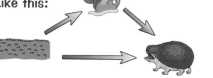

1) <u>FOOD WEBS</u> are made from lots of food chains joined together. Like this:

2) The hedgehog is a <u>primary consumer</u> and a <u>secondary consumer</u>.

3) This means it can get <u>energy</u> from lots of <u>different foods</u>.

A Change to One Bit of the Food Chain Can Affect the Rest of it

1) If <u>one part</u> of a <u>food chain changes</u>, it can <u>affect</u> the <u>whole</u> of the food chain.

2) For example:

Dandelions   Rabbits   Foxes

If all the <u>rabbits</u> in the food chain above get a <u>disease</u> and <u>die</u>:

- There might be <u>more dandelions</u> because there'd be nothing to eat them.

- There might be <u>fewer foxes</u> because they'd have less food to eat.

Practice Questions

1) What are <u>producers</u>?
2) What is a <u>trophic level</u>?

Pyramids of Biomass and Numbers

Pyramids of biomass and numbers are another way of showing what's going on in a food chain.

You Need to be able to Understand and Draw Pyramids of Biomass

1) Take a look at this food chain:

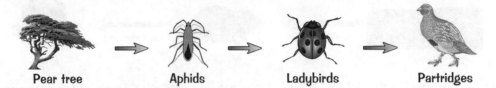

Pear tree → Aphids → Ladybirds → Partridges

2) This is a PYRAMID OF BIOMASS for the food chain:

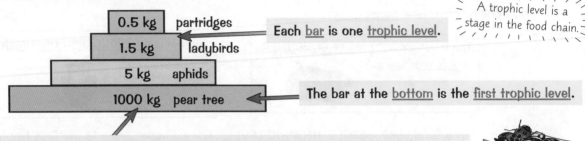

0.5 kg	partridges
1.5 kg	ladybirds
5 kg	aphids
1000 kg	pear tree

Each bar is one trophic level.

A trophic level is a stage in the food chain.

The bar at the bottom is the first trophic level.

The SIZE of each bar shows how much all the organisms would WEIGH if you dried them out. The posh way of saying this is 'each bar shows the dry mass of living material'.

In the pyramid above, the 'pear tree' bar is LONGER than the 'aphids' bar. This is because the pear tree weighs more than the aphids.

Pyramids of Biomass and Pyramids of Numbers can be Different Shapes

1) Each bar on a pyramid of numbers shows the NUMBER of organisms (not their mass).

2) Pyramids of BIOMASS are nearly always PYRAMID-SHAPED.

3) Pyramids of NUMBERS can be OTHER SHAPES.

4) Here's a pyramid of numbers for the food chain above:

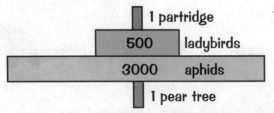

1 partridge
500 ladybirds
3000 aphids
1 pear tree

The 'aphids' bar on this pyramid is longer than the 'pear tree' bar. This is because one pear tree can feed lots of aphids.

Practice Questions

1) What does the size of each bar of a pyramid of biomass show?

2) "Pyramids of numbers are always pyramid-shaped." True or false?

Energy Transfer and Energy Flow

Every living thing needs energy. And we get it from food.

Energy From the Sun Passes Through the Food Chain

(1) Energy comes from the SUN.

(2) Plants use some of the sun's energy to make their own food. This is called PHOTOSYNTHESIS.

At each stage of the food chain energy is LOST:

1) As HEAT from respiration.

Respiration is a reaction that gives us energy.

2) By getting rid of undigested food. This is EGESTION.

3) By getting rid of waste products made in the body. This is EXCRETION.

HEAT LOSS

MATERIALS LOST IN ANIMAL'S WASTE

(3) Animals can get the Sun's energy by:

• EATING PLANTS.

• EATING OTHER ANIMALS that have eaten plants.

(4) • Waste products like faeces (poo) can start new food chains. For example, houseflies eat faeces.

• Some bits of animals and plants aren't eaten, like bones. These bits can also start new food chains.

You Need to Understand Data About Energy Flow

1) Take a look at this food chain:

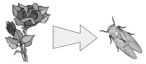 

A 'kJ' is a unit of energy.

rosebush: 80 000 kJ   greenfly: 10 000 kJ   ladybird: 900 kJ   bird: 40 kJ

2) The numbers show the amount of energy in the creatures at each level.

A trophic level is a stage in the food chain.

3) You can work out how much energy has been lost at each trophic level.

4) You just TAKE AWAY the energy in one trophic level from the energy in the previous trophic level. For example:

Energy lost at SECOND TROPHIC LEVEL	=	80 000 kJ — 10 000 kJ = 70 000 kJ
		rosebush greenfly

Practice Questions

1) Where does the energy in a food chain come from?

2) Give two ways in which energy is lost from a food chain.

Interactions Between Organisms

Organisms <u>interact</u> (affect each other) in <u>loads of different ways</u>...

Plants and Animals Compete for Resources

<u>Animals</u> compete for resources like:

- **SHELTER**
- **FOOD**
- **WATER**

<u>Plants</u> compete for resources like:

- **LIGHT**
- **WATER**
- **SOIL MINERALS**

1) Plants and animals compete for these things so they can <u>SURVIVE</u> and <u>REPRODUCE</u>.

2) <u>Animals</u> that are <u>similar</u> and live in the <u>same place</u> will <u>compete</u> for <u>resources</u>. This is because they'll need the <u>same things</u>. For example, the same food.

Competition Affects...

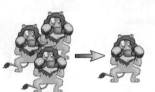

(1) <u>POPULATION SIZE</u>. <u>Lots of competition</u> could lead to <u>smaller populations</u>.

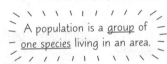

A population is a <u>group</u> of <u>one species</u> living in an area.

(2) <u>DISTRIBUTION</u> of organisms (where they live). Organisms might <u>move away</u> from <u>areas</u> where there's <u>strong competition</u>.

Some Species Need Other Species to Survive

1) Some species <u>need</u> other species to <u>survive</u>. This is called <u>INTERDEPENDENCE</u>.

2) <u>Parasitic relationships</u> and <u>mutualistic relationships</u> are examples of interdependence.

<u>PARASITIC RELATIONSHIPS</u>

1) <u>Parasites</u> live off a <u>host</u>. A host is another animal or plant.

2) Parasites <u>take</u> what they need to survive. They <u>don't</u> give anything <u>back</u>.

3) This <u>HURTS</u> the host.

<u>EXAMPLES:</u>

<u>TAPEWORMS</u> live inside animals. They get <u>food</u> from the animal, which can make the animal <u>ill</u>.

<u>FLEAS</u> get blood from dogs. Dogs just get bitten.

<u>MUTUALISTIC RELATIONSHIPS</u>

These are relationships that are <u>helpful</u> to <u>BOTH organisms</u>.

<u>EXAMPLES:</u>

<u>OXPECKER</u> birds are a "<u>CLEANER SPECIES</u>". They <u>eat harmful insects</u> that live on <u>buffalo</u>.

Some <u>INSECTS</u> carry <u>POLLEN</u> between <u>plants</u>. This allows the plants to <u>reproduce</u>. The insects drink the plant's <u>nectar</u> (a sugary juice).

Practice Questions

1) What resources do <u>animals</u> compete for?

2) Describe <u>one</u> example of a <u>parasitic relationship</u>.

Predators and Prey

School might be tough — but it's nothing compared to nature. For example, students don't get eaten...

Predators Eat Prey

A **PREDATOR** is an animal that hunts and eats other animals.

The **PREY** is the animal that gets hunted and eaten.

The Number of Prey Affects the Number of Predators

1) Populations of predators and prey go in **CYCLES**. Here's an example:

A population is a group of one species living in an area.

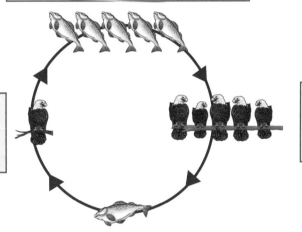

1) The population of FISH increases.

5) But now there aren't as many birds to eat the fish...

4) There aren't as many fish for the birds to eat. The population of BIRDS drops too.

2) There are more fish for the birds to eat. The population of BIRDS increases.

3) There are more birds to eat the fish. The population of FISH drops.

2) You can show cycles like the one above on graphs that look like this:

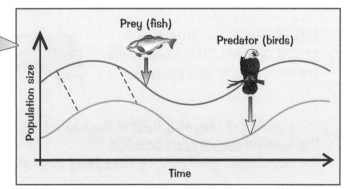

Practice Questions

1) What is a predator?
2) "Populations of predator and prey don't affect each other." True or false?

Module B2 — Understanding Our Environment

Adaptations of Predators and Prey

Predators and prey are so <u>awesome</u>, I figured you needed another page all about them. So here you are.

Predators and Prey are Well Adapted

1) <u>ADAPTATIONS</u> are features that help organisms to <u>compete</u> and <u>survive</u> (see next page).

2) <u>PREDATORS</u> are <u>adapted</u> to be good at <u>HUNTING</u>.

3) <u>PREY</u> are <u>adapted</u> so they're good at <u>NOT GETTING CAUGHT</u>.

Predators Are Adapted for Hunting Prey

1 Most predators have <u>BINOCULAR VISION</u>. This means their <u>eyes</u> are on the <u>front</u> of their head. It lets them see:
- <u>how far away</u> their prey is,
- <u>how big</u> their prey is.

2 Many predators only <u>BREED</u> when there's <u>LOTS</u> of <u>PREY</u> to feed their young.

3 Many predators <u>CHASE</u> their prey.

4 Some hunt in <u>TEAMS</u>.

5 Others <u>AMBUSH</u> (sneak up on) their prey.

Prey Are Adapted so They Don't Get Caught

1 Lots of prey have <u>EYES ON THE SIDE OF THEIR HEAD</u>. This means they can spot predators on both sides.

2 Some prey have <u>CRYPTIC COLOURING</u>. This makes it <u>harder</u> for predators to <u>see</u> prey.

For example, arctic hares are hard to see against the snow.

3 Other prey have <u>WARNING COLOURS</u>. This tells predators that the prey are <u>poisonous</u>.

4 Some prey <u>MIMIC</u> (look like) more <u>dangerous species</u>. This makes the prey <u>look dangerous</u> too.

5 Lots of prey live in <u>SHOALS</u> or <u>HERDS</u> (groups). This means there are more prey to <u>spot predators</u>.

6 Some groups of prey all <u>BREED</u> at the <u>SAME TIME</u>. This is called <u>synchronous breeding</u>. The <u>more babies</u> there are, the <u>more likely</u> some are to <u>survive</u>.

Practice Questions

1) What are <u>adaptations</u>?

2) How does <u>cryptic colouring</u> help prey avoid predators?

Adaptations to Dry Environments

There are <u>loads</u> of different kinds of <u>adaptations</u>. Some help organisms survive in <u>dry environments</u>.

Adaptations **Help Organisms Survive**

1) Organisms need <u>RESOURCES</u> like food and water.
   But they have to <u>COMPETE</u> with other organisms to get them.

2) If an organism is <u>ADAPTED</u> to its environment, it's <u>better</u> at <u>competing</u>.

3) This means it's <u>more likely</u> to:

<u>SURVIVE</u>   <u>REPRODUCE</u>   <u>PASS ON</u> its helpful adaptations
                                                        to its <u>offspring</u> (children).

Some Organisms **Are** Adapted **to Living in** Dry Environments

1) Some organisms live in <u>dry environments</u>. For example, the <u>desert</u>.

2) They have <u>adaptations</u> that <u>stop</u> them <u>losing water</u>.

3) These adaptations help them to <u>survive</u>.

Some Desert Plants...

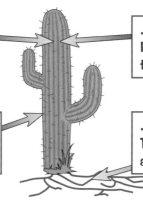

... are covered in a **THICK WAXY LAYER**. This is called a <u>cuticle</u>. It <u>seals water in</u>.

... have a **THICK STEM**. It <u>stores</u> water for when there's not much around.

... have **SPINES**. These lose less water than leaves.

... have **LONG ROOTS**. This means they can get as much water as possible.

Some Desert Animals...

... <u>DON'T</u> have <u>SWEAT GLANDS</u>. This means they can't lose water by sweating.

... make <u>urine</u> with very <u>little water</u> in it. This means they only lose a little water when they <u>wee</u>.

... spend lots of time <u>underground</u> where there's more water.

Practice Questions

1) "Organisms that are <u>adapted</u> to their environment are more likely to <u>die</u>." True or false?

2) Describe <u>one</u> adaptation of <u>plants</u> to dry environments.

3) Describe <u>one</u> adaptation of <u>animals</u> to dry environments.

Module B2 — Understanding Our Environment

Adaptations to Hot and Cold Environments

Yes it's another page on adaptations. Oh joy. Will the fun never end...

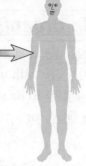

Surface Area is Important For Losing Heat

1) Your surface area is the area of your skin.

2) Animals with a BIG surface area will lose LOTS OF HEAT.

3) Animals with a SMALL surface area will lose LESS HEAT.

Animals that Live in Cold Places Need to Keep Their Body Heat

1) If you live somewhere COLD, you need to lose as LITTLE HEAT as possible.

2) Some animals have body adaptations that stop them losing heat. Some animals adapt their behaviour.

BODY ADAPTATIONS	ADAPTATIONS IN BEHAVIOUR
1) THICK FUR. This INSULATES the body. Insulates means traps heat in.	1) Some animals HIBERNATE (sleep) in the winter. This means they don't need to stay as warm.
2) A layer of BLUBBER (fat). This also insulates the body.	2) Some animals MIGRATE (move) to warmer places during the winter.
3) Small ears and a rounded shape. This gives them a SMALL SURFACE AREA. So they lose less heat.	

Your body is also called your anatomy. So body adaptations can also be called anatomical adaptations.

Animals that Live in Hot Places Need to Lose their Body Heat

1) If you live somewhere HOT, you need to lose as MUCH HEAT as possible.

2) You also need to stop yourself getting too hot in the first place. This is called reducing heat gain.

BODY ADAPTATIONS

Some animals have long tails or big ears. This gives them a LARGE SURFACE AREA. So they lose a lot of heat.

ADAPTATIONS IN BEHAVIOUR

1) Some animals spend the day UNDERGROUND. It's cooler here, so they don't get as hot.

2) They have BATHS. This helps them to lose heat.

Practice Questions

1) Give one adaptation of animals to cold environments.

2) Give one adaptation of animals to hot environments.

Evolution and Natural Selection

Evolution sounds like a tricky topic, but it's really not. It's just about how species change.

Natural Selection Explains Evolution

1) Evolution is where species change slowly over time.

2) NATURAL SELECTION explains evolution.
Here's how natural selection works:

EXAMPLE

Some foxes can see better than others.

> Living things are all a bit different. They VARY.

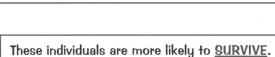

Some individuals are better at competing for resources. This means they're BETTER ADAPTED.

> These individuals are more likely to SURVIVE. This is called, 'SURVIVAL OF THE FITTEST'.

These individuals are also more likely to REPRODUCE. They pass on their useful adaptations to their offspring.

Lots of individuals end up with the useful adaptations. The species changes. This means it EVOLVES.

Adaptations Are Controlled by Genes

1) Adaptations are controlled by genes (see page 25).

2) Genes can be passed on from parents to their offspring.

3) Which means that adaptations can be passed on too.

Darwin Came Up With the Idea of Natural Selection

1) CHARLES DARWIN came up with the idea of natural selection. He called it his theory of evolution.

2) At first, lots of people DIDN'T AGREE with Darwin. This was sometimes because of their religion.

3) Other people had different theories about how evolution worked.

4) Most people agree with Darwin now though. Here's why:

- Lots of scientists have tested Darwin's ideas.

- His ideas explain lots of observations (things we see) in plants and animals.

Practice Questions

1) "Individuals who are better at competing for resources are better adapted." True or false?

2) Who came up with the idea of natural selection?

The Carbon Cycle

Carbon is pretty darn important. So it's a good thing it gets <u>recycled</u>. We wouldn't want it to run out on us...

Living Organisms Need Carbon

See page 29 for more on elements.

1) Plants and animals <u>take in CHEMICALS</u> from their environment as they <u>GROW</u>.

2) They <u>use ELEMENTS</u> from these chemicals to help them make <u>NEW TISSUES</u>. For example, skin and muscle.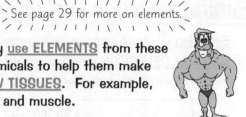

3) The most <u>important</u> elements they need are <u>CARBON</u> (see below) and <u>NITROGEN</u> (see next page).

The Carbon Cycle Shows How Carbon is Recycled

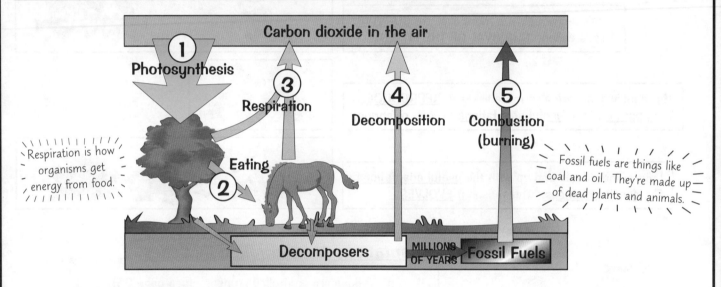

You need to learn these important points:

1) <u>Plants get carbon</u> from <u>carbon dioxide</u> in the <u>air</u>. They do this using <u>PHOTOSYNTHESIS</u>.

2) Carbon is passed from plants to animals when animals <u>EAT</u> the plants.

3) <u>RESPIRATION</u> releases carbon dioxide back into the <u>air</u>.

4) <u>Dead</u> plants and animals are broken down during <u>decomposition</u>.

   • When plants and animals <u>die</u> they're broken down by <u>DECOMPOSERS</u>.

   • Decomposers are <u>bacteria</u> and <u>fungi</u> in the soil.

   • They <u>release carbon dioxide</u> when they break down the dead material.

5) The <u>COMBUSTION</u> (burning) of <u>fossil fuels</u> also releases carbon dioxide into the air.

All this means that carbon is <u>recycled</u>. It can be <u>used again</u>.

Practice Questions

1) Where do <u>plants</u> get <u>carbon</u> from?

2) How is <u>carbon</u> passed from plants to animals?

The Nitrogen Cycle and Decomposition

Just like carbon, nitrogen is always being recycled...

Nitrogen is Recycled in the Nitrogen Cycle

1) About 78% of the atmosphere (air) is NITROGEN gas.

2) Plants and animals need nitrogen so they can make PROTEINS. They use the proteins to grow.

3) But they can't use the nitrogen in the atmosphere because it's very UNREACTIVE.

4) Plants get their nitrogen from nitrates in the soil. Nitrogen gets passed on to animals in the nitrogen cycle:

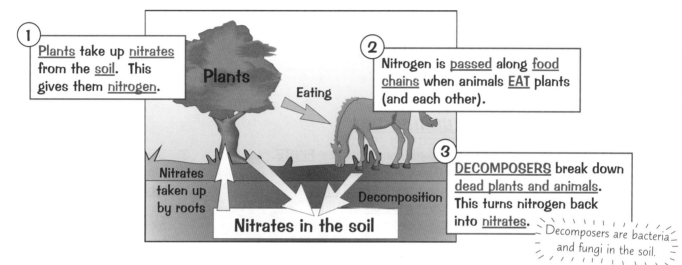

1 Plants take up nitrates from the soil. This gives them nitrogen.

Plants

Eating

2 Nitrogen is passed along food chains when animals EAT plants (and each other).

3 DECOMPOSERS break down dead plants and animals. This turns nitrogen back into nitrates.

Decomposers are bacteria and fungi in the soil.

Nitrates taken up by roots

Nitrates in the soil

Decomposition

Decomposition is Slower in Some Types of Soil

DECOMPOSITION is when decomposers break down dead material.

Waterlogged soils are soils that are soaked in water.

Decomposition is SLOWER in WATERLOGGED SOILS than in well-drained soils. This is because:

Decomposers need OXYGEN to work...

Well-drained soil

...but waterlogged soils don't have much oxygen.

Waterlogged soil

So decomposers don't work well in waterlogged soils.

Decomposition is SLOWER in ACIDIC SOILS than in neutral soils. This is because:

Neutral soil

Decomposers reproduce more slowly in acidic soils.

Acidic soil

Acidic soils can even kill decomposers.

Acidic soils have a low pH. Neutral soils have a pH of 7.

Practice Questions

1) Why do plants and animals need nitrogen?

2) Where do plants get nitrogen from?

Human Impact on the Environment

We'd be <u>stuffed</u> without the environment. But our <u>pollution</u> is damaging it.

The Human Population is Increasing

1) The <u>human population</u> is <u>getting bigger</u>.

2) It's getting bigger <u>EXPONENTIALLY</u> (faster and faster).

3) Populations get bigger when <u>more people</u> are <u>born</u> in a year <u>than die</u>.

4) The posh way of saying this is that populations grow when the <u>BIRTH RATE</u> is <u>HIGHER</u> than the <u>DEATH RATE</u>.

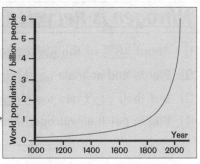

This graph shows that the human population is getting bigger.

Some Resources Are Running Out

Fossil fuels are coal, oil and natural gas.

1) <u>More people</u> use <u>more resources</u>.

2) Some resources are <u>FINITE</u>. This means they'll <u>run out</u> one day. <u>Fossil fuels</u> and <u>minerals</u> are finite resources.

3) Using more resources makes <u>more pollution</u>. For example, more <u>sewage</u> and <u>household waste</u>.

More Pollution is Causing...

ACID RAIN

1) When <u>fossil fuels</u> are burnt they give off <u>sulfur dioxide</u>.

2) Sulfur dioxide turns <u>rain</u> into <u>acid rain</u>.

3) Acid rain can <u>kill trees</u> and <u>fish</u>.

GLOBAL WARMING

When fossil fuels are burnt, they give off <u>carbon dioxide</u>. Carbon dioxide is a <u>greenhouse gas</u>.

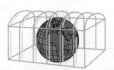

Greenhouse gases <u>trap heat</u>. This is heating up the Earth. It's called <u>global warming</u>.

Global warming could change the <u>weather</u>. This might make it <u>harder</u> for farmers to <u>grow food</u>.

PROBLEMS WITH OZONE

1) <u>CFCs</u> used to be found in <u>spray cans</u>.

2) They <u>break down the ozone layer</u>.

3) This lets <u>more UV rays</u> reach the Earth.

4) UV rays can cause <u>skin cancer</u>. More UV rays mean <u>more skin cancer</u>.

Practice Questions

1) Name <u>two</u> finite resources.

2) What problem can <u>sulfur dioxide</u> cause?

Human Impact on the Environment

Humans are <u>polluting</u> the planet — and we can <u>measure</u> just how badly we're doing it...

Indicator Species Can Be Used to Show Pollution

1) <u>Pollution</u> affects the <u>NUMBER</u> of <u>organisms</u> that can survive in a particular place.
   It also affects the <u>TYPE</u> of organisms that can survive.

2) Some species <u>ONLY live</u> in areas that <u>AREN'T</u> polluted. Others <u>ONLY live</u> in areas that <u>ARE</u> polluted.

3) These species are called <u>INDICATOR SPECIES</u>. They can <u>show</u> you if an <u>area</u> is <u>polluted</u> or <u>not</u>.
   Here are some examples:

	LICHEN	MAYFLY LARVAE	WATER LICE	RAT-TAILED MAGGOTS	SLUDGEWORMS
Indicator Species:					
Found where there's...	<u>clean air</u>	<u>clean water</u>	<u>polluted water</u>	<u>polluted water</u>	<u>polluted water</u>

You Can Measure Pollution

You can use <u>indicator species</u> to <u>MEASURE POLLUTION</u>. There are two ways to do it:

1) You could do a <u>SURVEY</u> to see if you <u>can</u> or can't <u>FIND</u> the indicator species in an area.

2) This tells you whether an area is <u>polluted or not</u>.

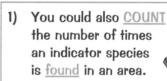

1) You could also <u>COUNT</u> the number of times an indicator species is <u>found</u> in an area.

2) This will tell you <u>HOW POLLUTED</u> the area is.

You can also measure pollution <u>DIRECTLY</u>. For example:

1) You can use scientific <u>INSTRUMENTS</u>, like a <u>pH meter</u>.

2) You can use information from <u>SATELLITES</u>.

Practice Questions

1) Name <u>one</u> indicator species that's only found where there's <u>clean air</u>.

2) Where are <u>sludgeworms</u> found?

3) "You can <u>only</u> measure pollution using indicator species." True or false?

Endangered Species

Loads of species are <u>endangered</u> these days. And in many cases, it's all <u>our fault</u>.

Some Species are Extinct, Many Species are Endangered

1) <u>EXTINCT</u> means there's <u>none</u> of a species left alive. For example, the <u>woolly mammoth</u>.

2) <u>ENDANGERED</u> species are species that are in danger of becoming <u>extinct</u>. For example, <u>pandas</u>.

3) Species are <u>more likely</u> to become extinct if there aren't enough:

HABITATS

It's hard to <u>find</u> <u>resources</u> like <u>food</u> and <u>shelter</u> if there aren't enough habitats. So the species will die out.

INDIVIDUALS

If there are only a few members of a species left, it'll be hard to find <u>mates</u>. Eventually the species will die out.

4) When the <u>environment changes</u>, some species <u>evolve</u> to cope (see p. 83). But many species become <u>extinct</u>.

There are Many Reasons Why Species Become Endangered

Species become <u>endangered</u> or <u>extinct</u> because of:

COMPETITION
Competition between species can make <u>populations</u> <u>smaller</u> (see page 78).

POLLUTION

CLIMATE CHANGE
The climate is changing because we're <u>burning</u> <u>fossil fuels</u>. Some species <u>can't cope</u> with these changes.

Climate means the conditions in an area, like the temperature and amount of rain and wind.

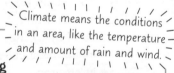

HABITAT DESTRUCTION
Lots of species' <u>homes</u> are being <u>destroyed</u>.

HUNTING ANIMALS

Practice Questions

1) What does <u>extinct</u> mean?

2) Why is a species more likely to become extinct if there aren't enough <u>habitats</u>?

3) "<u>Pollution</u> makes it more likely some species will become endangered." True or false?

Protecting Endangered Species

There are lots of ways we can make sure species <u>don't</u> become <u>extinct</u>.

There are <u>SIX</u> Main Ways to <u>Protect Endangered Species</u>

① EDUCATION PROGRAMMES

We can <u>teach people</u> how to protect endangered species.

② PROTECTED HABITATS

We can <u>protect important areas</u>.

③ LEGAL PROTECTION

We can make <u>laws</u> to protect species.

④ CAPTIVE BREEDING

We can breed endangered species in <u>zoos</u>. This is called <u>captive breeding</u>.

⑤ SEED BANKS

Plant seeds can be <u>stored</u> in seed banks. If the plants become <u>extinct</u>, new plants can be <u>grown</u> from the seeds.

⑥ ARTIFICIAL ECOSYSTEMS

We can make <u>somewhere</u> for species <u>to live</u>. This is called creating an <u>artificial ecosystem</u>.

Conservation Programmes <u>Help</u> Wildlife and Humans

1) <u>CONSERVATION PROGRAMMES</u> are where people <u>protect species</u>.

2) They <u>help endangered species</u> to survive. They also <u>help humans</u>. For example they can:

GIVE US FOOD FOR THE FUTURE

We <u>eat plants and animals</u>. If we look after them, we'll still have plenty to eat in the future.

GIVE US MEDICINES FOR THE FUTURE

Lots of <u>medicines</u> come from <u>plants</u>. If we protect them we might find new medicines in the future.

REDUCE DAMAGE TO FOOD CHAINS

If we protect <u>one species</u> in a food chain, it might help <u>other species</u> survive too.

PROTECT OUR CULTURES

Some species are important to people's <u>culture</u>. Protecting the species helps protect the culture too.

Practice Questions

1) Give <u>three</u> ways that species can be protected.

2) "Species are never protected because they're important to a <u>people's culture</u>." True or false?

Sustainable Development

It's not all doom and gloom... if we do things <u>sustainably</u> we'll be OK.

You Need to Know All About Sustainable Development

SUSTAINABLE DEVELOPMENT means providing for the needs of today's increasing population <u>without</u> harming the environment.

This just means using resources without using them up or damaging the environment.

1) <u>SUSTAINABLE RESOURCES</u> can be <u>taken</u> from the environment <u>without</u> them <u>running out</u>.

2) <u>Fish</u> and <u>wood</u> can be sustainable resources. Here's how:

There are <u>FISHING QUOTAS</u>. These stop boats catching too many fish.

When logging companies cut down trees they have to <u>PLANT NEW ONES</u>.

3) <u>EDUCATION</u> helps make sustainable development work. If people <u>know</u> about the problems, they might <u>help</u>. For example, by <u>not buying</u> endangered species of fish.

Some Whale Species are Endangered

1) Whales have <u>COMMERCIAL VALUE</u>. This means they can be used to <u>make money</u>.

LIVING WHALES

Make money by being a <u>tourist attraction</u>.

DEAD WHALES

Can be used to make <u>meat</u>, <u>oil</u> and <u>cosmetics</u> (make up). These can be sold.

2) But using whales like this means some species are <u>nearly EXTINCT</u>.

3) Some whales are kept in <u>CAPTIVITY</u> (in places like zoos).

4) People have <u>different views</u> about this.

The whales don't have much space. I don't think that's fair.

I think it's wrong that captive whales are used to entertain us.

I don't think it's right that the whales have lost their freedom.

Our research on captive whales helps to conserve them.

We can breed from captive whales and release their kids into the wild. I think this is great because it helps conserve them.

5) <u>Where</u> whale species are <u>found in the wild</u> often depends on what they <u>eat</u>.

Practice Questions

1) What does <u>sustainable development</u> mean?

2) Suggest how we can limit the amount of <u>fish</u> we catch.

3) Give <u>two</u> ways that <u>dead whales</u> can be used to make <u>money</u>.

The Earth's Structure

This page is all about what the Earth is like inside, and how scientists study it...

The Earth has a Crust, a Mantle and a Core

1) The Earth is a SPHERE (a ball shape).
2) It's made up of lots of different layers:

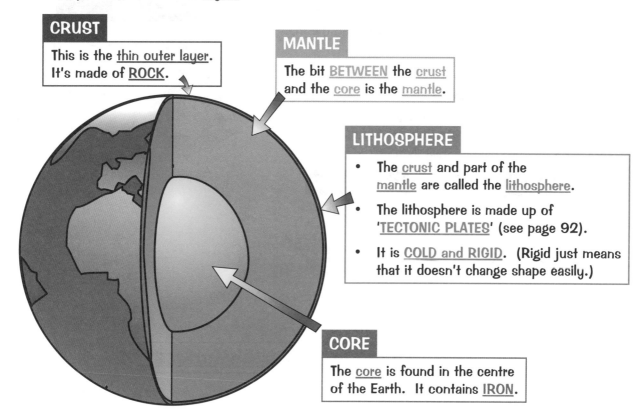

CRUST

This is the thin outer layer. It's made of ROCK.

MANTLE

The bit BETWEEN the crust and the core is the mantle.

LITHOSPHERE

- The crust and part of the mantle are called the lithosphere.
- The lithosphere is made up of 'TECTONIC PLATES' (see page 92).
- It is COLD and RIGID. (Rigid just means that it doesn't change shape easily.)

CORE

The core is found in the centre of the Earth. It contains IRON.

Scientists Study What's Inside the Earth

1) It's difficult to study inside the Earth because the crust is TOO THICK to drill through.
2) Scientists use SEISMIC WAVES (shock waves) to study the inside of the Earth.

Seismic waves are made by earthquakes or by setting off big explosions at the Earth's surface.

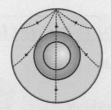

These waves can travel through the Earth.

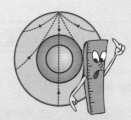

Scientists measure where the waves leave the Earth. They can then work out what the Earth is like inside.

Practice Questions

1) Which layer of the Earth is made up of the crust and part of the mantle?
2) What type of waves are used to study the inside of the Earth?

Tectonic Plates

The Earth's surface is made up of large lumps of rock called <u>tectonic plates</u>.

The Earth's Surface <u>is</u> Broken <u>into</u> Big Pieces

1) The Earth's surface is <u>broken</u> into <u>large pieces of rock</u> called <u>TECTONIC PLATES</u>.

2) These tectonic plates <u>FLOAT</u> on the <u>mantle</u>.

3) They float because they are <u>LESS DENSE</u> than the mantle.

4) <u>CONTINENTS</u> are big areas of land like <u>Africa</u>.

5) The <u>continents</u> are made from the tectonic plates.

6) The plates move very <u>SLOWLY</u> — about <u>2.5 cm per year</u>.

7) This means it's taken <u>millions of years</u> for the continents to move to where they are today.

8) When the tectonic plates move they can cause...

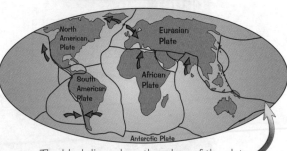

The black lines show the edges of the plates.

VOLCANOES

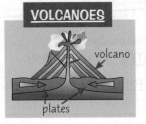

EARTHQUAKES

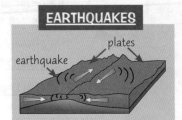

It's Taken a Long Time to Explain the <u>Earth's Surface</u>

Scientists tried for <u>AGES</u> to work out <u>why</u> the surface of the Earth is like it is.

Because tectonic plates move <u>so SLOWLY</u> scientists <u>didn't</u> think they were <u>moving</u> at all.

So they came up with loads of <u>other IDEAS</u> to <u>explain</u> the Earth's surface. But <u>none</u> of them were quite right...

There <u>is</u> Loads of <u>Evidence</u> For Plate Tectonics

1) For scientists to <u>agree</u> on an idea there has to be enough <u>EVIDENCE</u> to back it up.

2) For <u>plate tectonics</u> there was <u>loads</u> of evidence.

3) Scientists have <u>studied</u> and <u>talked about</u> plate tectonics a lot and now accept the idea as being <u>correct</u>.

Evidence is something that helps to prove an idea.

Practice Questions

1) How <u>fast</u> do tectonic plates move?

2) What do you have to have for scientists to <u>agree on an idea</u>?

Volcanoes

Volcanoes are made where two tectonic plates meet.

Volcanoes are Made by Molten Rock

1) MOLTEN ROCK is rock that has been MELTED.

2) VOLCANOES are made when molten rock breaks through the Earth's crust.

When molten rock erupts from a volcano it's called LAVA.

When molten rock is below the surface of the Earth it's called MAGMA.

3) Scientists study volcanoes to guess when they'll next happen.

4) They also study volcanoes to find information about what's inside the Earth.

Lava Can be Runny or Thick

- Some volcanoes make RUNNY lava.
- The eruption is fairly safe.

- Other volcanoes make THICK lava.
- This eruption is explosive which is really DANGEROUS.

1) It might seem silly that some people choose to live CLOSE to volcanoes, but it can be useful.

2) For example, ash from volcanoes makes the soil great for FARMING.

Rocks are Made from Cooling Magma

1) Rocks are made from molten rock that COOLS DOWN and goes HARD.

2) The molten rock turns into CRYSTALS as it cools down.

Some rocks cool QUICKLY above ground. They form SMALL crystals.

Some rocks cool SLOWLY underground. They form BIG crystals.

Practice Questions

1) What is molten rock called when it erupts from a volcano?

2) Why might someone choose to live near a volcano?

3) If a rock cools quickly, will the crystals be big or small?

Limestone and Marble

Limestone and marble are both really useful <u>building materials</u>.

Limestone and Marble are made from Calcium Carbonate

1) <u>LIMESTONE</u> and <u>MARBLE</u> are both types of rock.

2) They are made from the chemical <u>CALCIUM CARBONATE</u>.

3) Even though they're both made from calcium carbonate they're <u>NOT</u> the <u>same</u>.

4) For example, <u>marble</u> is <u>MUCH HARDER</u> than <u>limestone</u>.

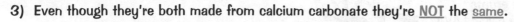

5) <u>GRANITE</u> is another type of rock. It's even <u>harder</u> than marble.

6) Limestone, marble and granite are all used as <u>BUILDING MATERIALS</u>.

Limestone can Break Down when it's Heated

1) Calcium carbonate <u>changes</u> into <u>two NEW substances</u> when it's <u>HEATED</u>.

2) This is called <u>THERMAL DECOMPOSITION</u>.

3) If you <u>HEAT calcium carbonate</u>, you get <u>CALCIUM OXIDE</u> and <u>CARBON DIOXIDE</u>.

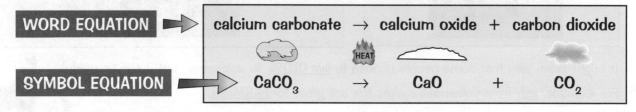

WORD EQUATION → calcium carbonate → calcium oxide + carbon dioxide

SYMBOL EQUATION → $CaCO_3$ → CaO + CO_2

Removing Rocks Can Damage the Environment

Rocks are removed from the ground by <u>MINING</u> or <u>QUARRYING</u>. This can cause problems, for example:

Mining makes <u>dust</u> and a lot of <u>noise</u>.

It <u>uses up land</u> and <u>destroys wildlife</u>.

Shhhhh.

Moving rock increases traffic which can cause <u>noise and pollution</u>.

It costs <u>money</u> to make mines look <u>pretty again</u>.

Practice Questions

1) Which is the <u>hardest</u> rock, <u>limestone</u>, <u>marble</u> or <u>granite</u>?

2) True or false: <u>calcium carbonate</u> + <u>calcium oxide</u> → <u>carbon dioxide</u>

3) Give two <u>problems</u> with <u>removing rocks</u> from the ground.

Construction Materials

Construction materials are materials that are used to make things like buildings or roads.

Aluminium and Iron Come from Rocks

1) Rocks with a lot of METAL in them are called ORES.

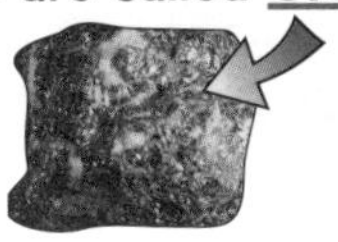

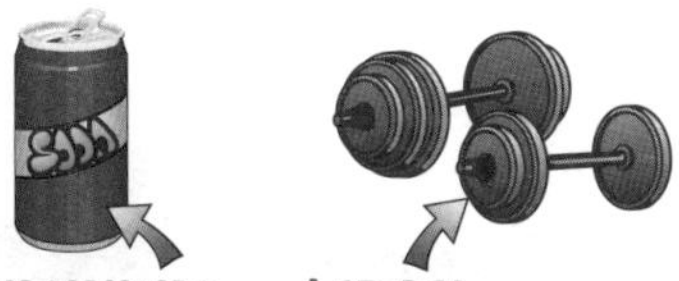

2) ALUMINIUM and IRON are both metals found in ores.

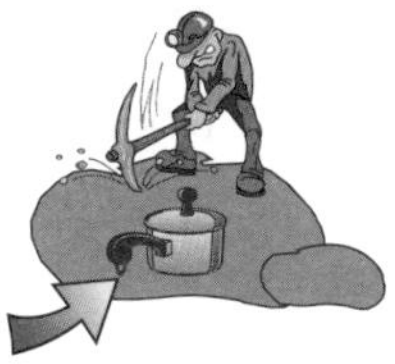

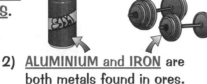

3) Metals can be REMOVED from their ores and used as CONSTRUCTION MATERIALS.

Glass and Bricks are Made from Other Materials

1) When SAND is heated it becomes GLASS.

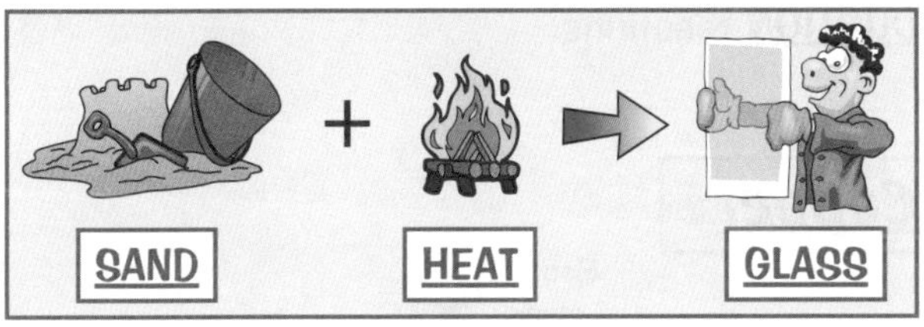
SAND
+
HEAT
GLASS

2) BRICKS are made from CLAY.

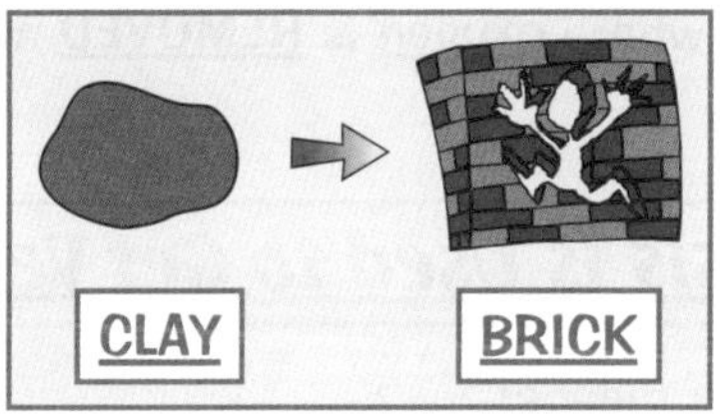
CLAY
BRICK

3) Bricks and glass are both used as CONSTRUCTION MATERIALS.

Limestone and Clay are Heated to Make Cement

1) Limestone can be used to make CEMENT and CONCRETE.

Limestone is heated with CLAY to make CEMENT.

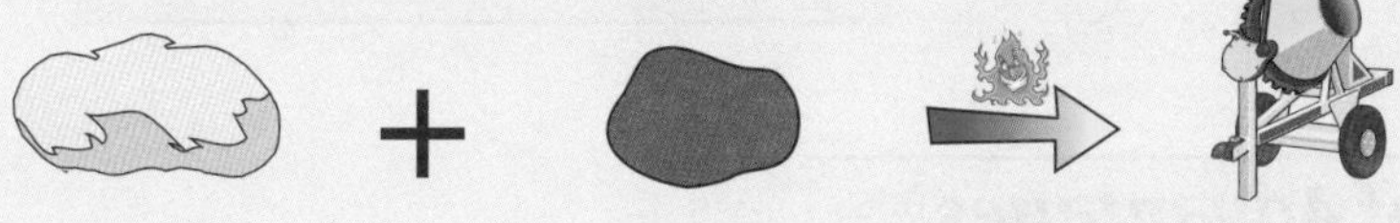

Gravel is sometimes called AGGREGATE.

To make CONCRETE mix CEMENT with SAND, WATER and GRAVEL. The mixture has to be left to SET.

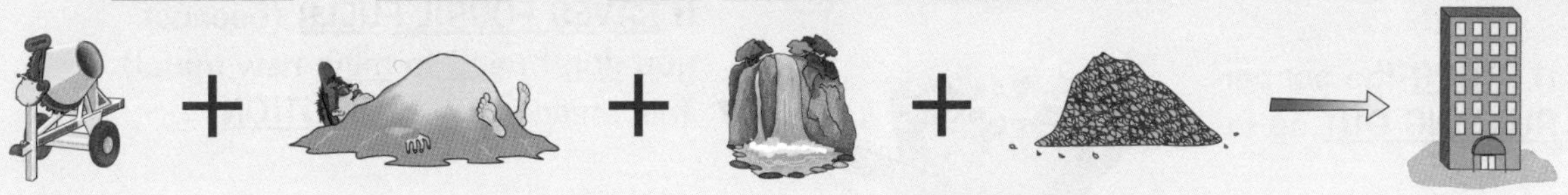

2) Concrete can be made stronger by setting it around steel.
3) This is called REINFORCED CONCRETE.
4) It's known as a COMPOSITE material.

Composite just means made up of different things.

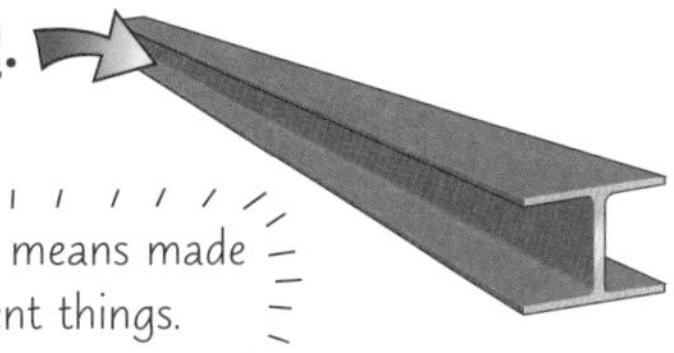

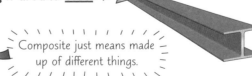

Practice Questions

1) Where do aluminium and iron come from?
2) How do you make glass?
3) What do you add to cement to make concrete?

Extracting Pure Copper

Here's a lovely page about <u>copper</u> and how it's made <u>pure</u>. Pure means <u>without</u> any <u>OTHER</u> <u>substances</u> in it.

Copper <u>is</u> Dug out of the Ground as a <u>Copper Ore</u>

1) Rocks with copper in are known as <u>COPPER ORES</u>.

2) Sometimes the copper is <u>joined</u> to <u>OXYGEN</u> in these ores.

3) <u>Oxygen</u> can be <u>REMOVED</u> from the copper by <u>heating</u> it with <u>CARBON</u>.

copper and oxygen + carbon + heat → copper + carbon and oxygen

4) Reactions where <u>oxygen</u> is <u>REMOVED</u> are called <u>REDUCTION</u> reactions.

Electrolysis <u>is</u> Used to Get <u>Very Pure Copper</u>

1) <u>Electrolysis</u> means:

> "<u>SPLITTING UP WITH ELECTRICITY</u>".

2) It's used to get <u>pure copper</u>.

3) You need to be able to <u>label the equipment</u> used to make copper pure.

It's OK, you don't have to know what any of the labels mean for the exam. Phew.

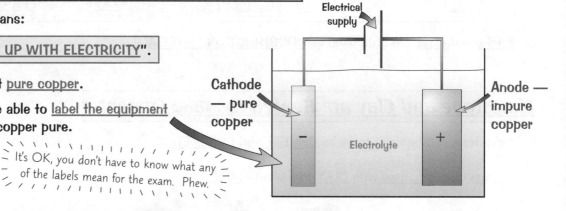

Electrical supply

Cathode — pure copper

Anode — impure copper

Electrolyte

Recycling Copper Has Lots of <u>Advantages...</u>

Here's why recycling is a <u>good idea</u>:

It <u>STOPS</u> the copper <u>RUNNING OUT</u> so fast.

It <u>SAVES FOSSIL FUELS</u> (because you <u>don't</u> need to <u>mine</u> new metal). This means <u>LESS POLLUTION</u>.

It takes <u>LESS</u> energy to <u>RECYCLE copper</u> than to <u>MINE and EXTRACT</u> <u>more copper</u>.

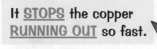

...but also some <u>Disadvantages</u>

- It can be <u>hard</u> to get people to sort and recycle their <u>waste metal</u>.

- You have to <u>sort out</u> the <u>copper</u> from all the other waste metal — which takes <u>time</u> and <u>energy</u>.

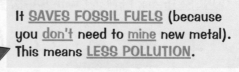

Practice Questions

1) What is the reaction where <u>oxygen is removed</u> called?
2) Give two <u>advantages</u> of <u>recycling copper</u>.

Module C2 — Chemical Resources

Alloys

Metals are pretty <u>useful</u> on their own. But sometimes mixing them together makes them <u>even better</u>.

An Alloy is a Mixture of Substances

1) An <u>ALLOY</u> is a <u>MIXTURE</u> of two or more <u>metals</u>. Or it can be a <u>MIXTURE</u> of a <u>metal</u> and a <u>non-metal</u>.

metal   another metal

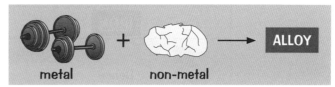

metal   non-metal

2) Alloys sometimes have <u>PROPERTIES</u> that are <u>different</u> from the metals they are <u>made from</u>.

3) For example, the alloy might be <u>LIGHTER</u>.

4) This can make the alloy <u>more USEFUL</u> than the <u>pure metal</u>.

vs.

Properties of metals are <u>what they're like</u>. For example, strong or hard.

Steel is an Alloy of Iron and Carbon

1) <u>STEEL</u> is made from <u>IRON</u> and <u>CARBON</u>. It's a very <u>useful alloy</u>.

2) Steel is <u>HARDER</u> than iron.

3) Steel is <u>STRONGER</u> than iron.

There's more on this on the next page.

4) Steel is much <u>less likely to RUST</u> than iron.

5) It's used to make <u>bridges</u>, <u>engine parts</u>, <u>cutlery</u>, <u>cars</u>...

Brass, Bronze, Solder and Amalgam are also Alloys

ALLOY	METALS IT'S MADE FROM	USES
BRASS	COPPER and ZINC	musical instruments door decorations coins
SOLDER	LEAD and TIN	To <u>join</u> electrical <u>wires</u> together.
AMALGAM	MERCURY	In <u>dentistry</u> to make <u>tooth fillings</u>.

Practice Questions

1) What is an <u>alloy</u>?
2) What metals is <u>solder</u> made from? Give one <u>use</u> of solder.

Iron and Aluminium

Iron and aluminium are two more metals which are really useful.

The Properties of Metals are Very Important

You need to know what IRON and ALUMINIUM are like...

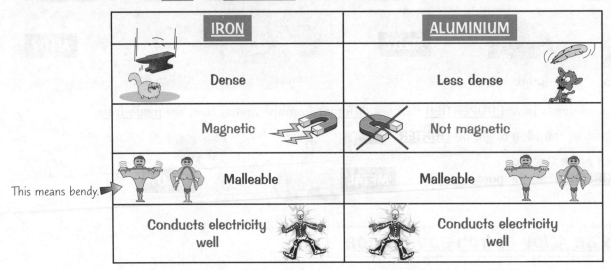

IRON	ALUMINIUM
Dense	Less dense
Magnetic	Not magnetic
Malleable	Malleable
Conducts electricity well	Conducts electricity well

This means bendy.

Corrosion is a Reaction that Destroys Metals

Iron Corrodes Easily

1) Corrosion of iron is called RUSTING.

2) Rusting only happens when OXYGEN (from the air) and WATER are around.

iron + oxygen + water → hydrated iron(III) oxide

Rust

3) Rusting is an OXIDATION reaction. (Oxidation is when oxygen is added.)

4) If the water is SALTY or ACIDIC (for example, in acid rain), rusting will be FASTER.

Aluminium Doesn't Corrode when it's Wet

1) When aluminium reacts with oxygen a layer of ALUMINIUM OXIDE is formed on the surface.

2) The aluminium oxide STOPS oxygen getting to the aluminium.

3) So the aluminium can't corrode.

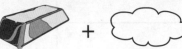

aluminium + oxygen → layer of aluminium oxide

Practice Questions

1) Which is more dense — iron or aluminium?

2) What is made when iron reacts with oxygen and water?

Module C2 — Chemical Resources

Building Cars

There are <u>loads of different materials</u> in cars, and they all have <u>different uses</u>.

Cars *Can be Made from* **Aluminium** *or* **Steel**

ALUMINIUM	VS.	STEEL
lighter		heavier
corrodes less		corrodes more easily
costs more		cheaper

You Need Various Materials *to Build* Different Bits *of a Car*

MATERIAL	PROPERTIES	USE
Steel	<u>Strong</u> and <u>malleable</u> (bendy).	Good for the <u>bodywork</u>.
Aluminium	<u>Strong</u> and <u>light</u>.	Used for <u>parts of the engine</u> to make it <u>lighter</u>.
Copper	<u>Malleable</u> and <u>conducts electricity</u>.	It's great for <u>electrical wiring</u>.
Glass	<u>Transparent</u> (<u>see through</u>).	<u>Windscreens</u> and <u>windows</u>.
Plastics	<u>Light</u>, <u>hard-wearing</u> and <u>doesn't conduct electricity</u>.	<u>Doors</u>, <u>dashboards</u> and for <u>covering electrical wires</u>.
Fibres	Lasts a <u>long time</u>. <u>Soft</u>.	Used to <u>cover</u> the <u>seats and floor</u>.

Recycling Cars **Has Advantages** *and* **Disadvantages**

New <u>laws</u> mean that you have to be able to <u>RECYCLE MOST</u> of a car. This has <u>advantages</u> and <u>disadvantages</u>.

ADVANTAGES
• It saves <u>NATURAL RESOURCES</u>
• It saves <u>MONEY</u>
• It means <u>LANDFILLS</u> are used <u>LESS</u>

DISADVANTAGES
• The <u>non-metal bits</u> of a car have to be <u>SEPARATED</u> first.
• Sorting out different types of plastic <u>costs a lot</u>.

Practice Questions

1) Which would be <u>cheaper</u>, a car made out of <u>aluminium</u> or a car made out of <u>steel</u>?

2) Name <u>two advantages</u> of <u>recycling</u> the materials used to make cars.

Acids and Bases

You'll find acids and bases at home, in industry and in the lab.

Universal Indicator Shows pH

1) If a substance has a pH of LESS THAN 7 it's an ACID.
2) If a substance has a pH of MORE THAN 7 it's a BASE.
3) A base that dissolves in water is called an ALKALI.

Very strong acid   Very strong alkali

pH 0   1   2   3   4   5   6   7   8   9   10   11   12   13   14

ACIDS   **ALKALIS**

pH less than 7.   pH more than 7.

NEUTRAL

pH of 7.   Pure water is neutral.

To FIND the pH of a SOLUTION:

*   Add a drop of UNIVERSAL INDICATOR.
*   Compare the colour it turns to the colour chart above.
*   This will tell you its pH.

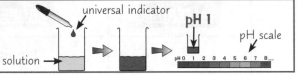

universal indicator

pH 1

pH scale

solution

pH 0 1 2 3 4 5 6 7 8...

Litmus Paper can Show if Something is an Acid or an Alkali

1) LITMUS PAPER is a special kind of paper that shows whether something is an ACID or an ALKALI.
2) It comes in red and blue. You just put the litmus paper in your solution.

If the RED paper turns BLUE then the solution is ALKALINE.

If the BLUE paper turns RED then the solution is ACIDIC.

When an Acid and Base React, They Make a Salt and Water

When you react an ACID with a BASE you get a SALT and WATER:

Salts aren't always like the salt you put on chips.

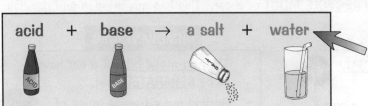

acid   +   base   →   a salt   +   water

The salt and water are NEUTRAL.
So it's called a NEUTRALISATION reaction.

Practice Questions

1) What colour would blue litmus paper be in an acidic solution?
2) What do you get if you react an acid and a base?

Reactions of Acids

Remember, <u>neutralisation</u> is an <u>acid</u> and a <u>base</u> reacting to give a <u>salt</u> and <u>water</u> (acid + base → salt + water).

Learn These Three Reactions of Acids

1) <u>Metal oxides</u>, <u>metal hydroxides</u> and <u>metal carbonates</u> are all <u>BASES</u>.

2) This means they will <u>neutralise acids</u> to make a <u>SALT</u> and <u>WATER</u>.

    acid + metal **OXIDE**   →   a salt + water

    acid + metal **HYDROXIDE** →   a salt + water

    acid + metal **CARBONATE** →   a salt + water + carbon dioxide

All of the reactions make a <u>SALT</u> and <u>WATER</u>.

This one's a bit different — you get <u>CARBON DIOXIDE</u> too.

The Metal and Acid Decide What the Salt Will Be

1) <u>Hydrochloric acid</u> gives a salt called a <u>CHLORIDE</u>.

Don't forget the <u>CARBON DIOXIDE</u> for the carbonate reaction.

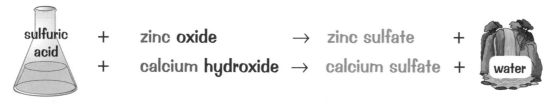

hydrochloric acid + copper **oxide** → copper chloride + water
+ sodium **hydroxide** → sodium chloride + water
+ sodium **carbonate** → sodium chloride + water + carbon dioxide

Here are the <u>SALTS</u>. Here's the <u>WATER</u>.

2) <u>Sulfuric acid</u> gives a salt called a <u>SULFATE</u>.

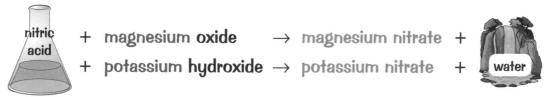

sulfuric acid + zinc **oxide** → zinc sulfate + water
+ calcium **hydroxide** → calcium sulfate + water

3) <u>Nitric acid</u> gives a salt called a <u>NITRATE</u>.

nitric acid + magnesium **oxide** → magnesium nitrate + water
+ potassium **hydroxide** → potassium nitrate + water

4) <u>Phosphoric acid</u> gives a salt called a <u>PHOSPHATE</u>.

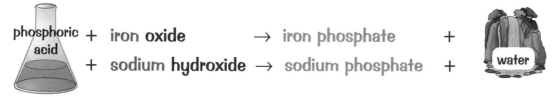

phosphoric acid + iron **oxide** → iron phosphate + water
+ sodium **hydroxide** → sodium phosphate + water

Practice Questions

1) What <u>three</u> things are made when an <u>acid</u> reacts with a <u>metal carbonate</u>?
2) What <u>salt</u> is made when <u>sulfuric acid</u> reacts with <u>calcium hydroxide</u>?

Fertilisers

Fertilisers make crops grow <u>bigger</u> and <u>faster</u>.

Fertilisers *Help to Make Healthy Crops*

1) There are some chemicals that plants <u>need</u> in order to grow properly.

2) These are called <u>ESSENTIAL ELEMENTS</u>.

NITROGEN	POTASSIUM	PHOSPHORUS
N	K	P

3) <u>FERTILISERS</u> can be used to make sure plants <u>get</u> these elements.

4) Using fertilisers increases the <u>CROP YIELD</u>.

5) The crop yield is just the <u>AMOUNT of crop grown</u>.

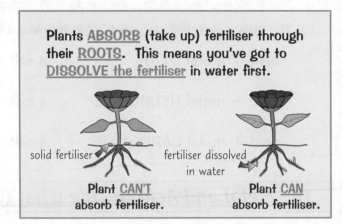

Plants <u>ABSORB</u> (take up) fertiliser through their <u>ROOTS</u>. This means you've got to <u>DISSOLVE the fertiliser</u> in water first.

solid fertiliser   fertiliser dissolved in water

Plant <u>CAN'T</u> absorb fertiliser.   Plant <u>CAN</u> absorb fertiliser.

Fertilisers *are Really Useful...*

The <u>POPULATION</u> of the world is <u>increasing</u> — there are more and more people to <u>feed</u>.

So we need to grow <u>more</u> <u>food</u> to feed everyone.

Fertilisers <u>INCREASE</u> crop yield, so <u>we can feed MORE people</u>.

...But They Can Cause Big Problems

1) If we use <u>too much</u> fertiliser we could <u>POLLUTE</u> our <u>WATER SUPPLIES</u>.

2) Fertilisers can also damage the <u>environment</u> by causing <u>EUTROPHICATION</u>:

Fertilisers can end up in <u>lakes</u> and <u>rivers</u>.

They can <u>CHANGE</u> the <u>underwater ENVIRONMENT</u>.

So pretty much <u>everything</u> in the river <u>DIES</u> (including fish and insects).

Practice Questions

1) Name the <u>three essential elements</u> that plants need in order to grow.

2) Give <u>one problem</u> caused by <u>fertilisers</u>.

Module C2 — Chemical Resources

Making Fertilisers

Ammonium nitrate is a good <u>fertiliser</u>. You can make it from a few simple chemicals.

Ammonia *Can be Used to Make* Fertilisers

1) You can make fertilisers from an <u>ACID</u> and an <u>ALKALI</u>.

2) The reaction is called a <u>NEUTRALISATION REACTION</u>.

3) <u>AMMONIA</u> (NH_3) is usually used as the <u>alkali</u>.

Making Fertilisers *in the Lab*

1) You can <u>make</u> most fertilisers using an <u>experiment</u> called a <u>TITRATION</u>.

2) Just choose the right <u>ACID</u> and <u>ALKALI</u> to get the <u>FERTILISER</u> you want.

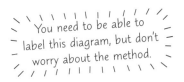
You need to be able to label this diagram, but don't worry about the method.

measuring cylinder to measure the alkali →

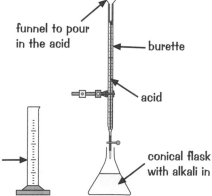
funnel to pour in the acid
burette
acid
conical flask with alkali in

The <u>Name</u> *of a Fertiliser Comes from the* <u>Acid</u> *and the* <u>Alkali Used</u>

1) You might have to <u>NAME</u> some <u>FERTILISERS</u> in the exam. Learn these ones and you'll be sorted...

ammonium nitrate   ammonium phosphate   urea   ammonium sulfate

2) If you need to know the <u>ESSENTIAL ELEMENT</u> that's in a fertiliser check the <u>FORMULA</u>.

- If it's got an <u>N</u> then it's got <u>NITROGEN</u> in it.
- If it's got a <u>K</u> then it's got <u>POTASSIUM</u> in it.
- If it's got a <u>P</u> then it's got <u>PHOSPHORUS</u> in it.

3) In the exam you might have to name the <u>acid</u> and the <u>alkali</u> needed to <u>make</u> a fertiliser. For example:

If the fertiliser starts with 'AMMONI' the alkali used to make it is ammonia.

AMMONIUM NITRATE

If the fertiliser ends with 'NITR' the acid used to make it is nitric acid.

AMMONIA   NITRIC ACID

You could get asked about other fertilisers too. Just look at the <u>name</u> closely and find a chemical which sounds the same.

Practice Questions

1) What is the <u>essential element</u> in the fertiliser NH_4NO_3?
2) What is the <u>alkali</u> used to make <u>ammonium sulfate</u> fertiliser?

The Haber Process

The <u>Haber process</u> is used to make <u>ammonia</u> (NH_3). Ammonia is used to make <u>fertilisers</u>.

Nitrogen _and Hydrogen_ are Needed to Make Ammonia

1) <u>Ammonia</u> is made from <u>NITROGEN</u> and <u>HYDROGEN</u>.

2) Here is the <u>WORD EQUATION</u> for the reaction: ➡ nitrogen + hydrogen ⇌ ammonia

3) This is what it means...

Nitrogen and hydrogen can <u>react</u> to make <u>AMMONIA</u>.

can react to make...

The <u>two-way arrow</u> means that the reaction is <u>REVERSIBLE</u> — it can go in both directions.

nitrogen + hydrogen ⇌ ammonia

can break down to make...

Ammonia can <u>break down</u> to give <u>NITROGEN</u> and <u>HYDROGEN</u>.

4) You need to know the <u>balanced symbol equation</u> too: ➡ $N_2 + 3H_2 \rightleftharpoons 2NH_3$

The Haber Process is a _Reversible Reaction_

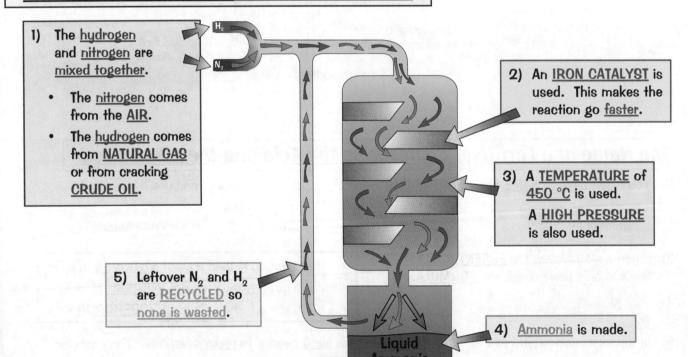

1) The <u>hydrogen</u> and <u>nitrogen</u> are <u>mixed together</u>.

- The <u>nitrogen</u> comes from the <u>AIR</u>.
- The <u>hydrogen</u> comes from <u>NATURAL GAS</u> or from cracking <u>CRUDE OIL</u>.

2) An <u>IRON CATALYST</u> is used. This makes the reaction go <u>faster</u>.

3) A <u>TEMPERATURE</u> of <u>450 °C</u> is used.
   A <u>HIGH PRESSURE</u> is also used.

5) Leftover N_2 and H_2 are <u>RECYCLED</u> so <u>none is wasted</u>.

4) <u>Ammonia</u> is made.

Liquid Ammonia

Ammonia Is _Really Useful_

<u>Ammonia</u> is used to <u>MAKE</u>:

NITRIC ACID

FERTILISERS

Practice Questions

1) Where does the <u>nitrogen</u> come from in the Haber process?
2) Write the <u>balanced symbol equation</u> for the Haber process.

The Cost of Production

In industry it's really important to <u>keep costs down</u> so that the business can make <u>money</u>.

The Cost of Making a New Substance Depends on Several Things

There are <u>FIVE</u> main things that affect the <u>COST</u> of making a new substance.

1 PRICE OF ENERGY

 The <u>PRICE of energy</u> is how much money is spent on <u>electricity</u> and <u>gas</u>.

 If a reaction needs a <u>high temperature</u> or <u>pressure</u>, <u>more energy</u> is needed and it'll <u>COST MORE</u>.

2 COST OF STARTING MATERIALS

- <u>Starting materials</u> are the materials used to <u>MAKE</u> a product.

- Costs can be kept low by <u>recycling</u> any <u>materials</u> that haven't reacted.

3 WAGES (LABOUR COSTS)

 Everyone who works for a company has got to be <u>paid</u>.

This is called automation.

Using <u>machines</u> cuts the number of <u>people needed</u>. This cuts <u>costs</u>.

4 EQUIPMENT (PLANT COSTS)

How much <u>equipment</u> costs depends on the <u>conditions</u> it has to cope with.

It costs <u>more</u> to make something that has to work in <u>HIGH</u> pressures or <u>temperatures</u>.

5 HOW QUICKLY THE SUBSTANCE CAN BE MADE

The <u>faster</u> a reaction goes, the <u>faster</u> the new material will be <u>made</u> and the <u>less</u> it costs.

To make a reaction faster you can use a <u>catalyst</u>.

Catalysts will <u>speed up</u> the reaction. This means the costs will go <u>down</u>.

But it will cost money to <u>buy</u> the catalyst in the first place.

Practice Questions

1) Do <u>high temperature</u> reactions cost more or less?
2) What will a <u>catalyst</u> do to the <u>speed</u> of a reaction?
3) What are <u>starting materials</u>?

Salt

Mmmm... <u>Salt</u>. Chips just wouldn't be the same without it.

Salt is Mined from Underground

1) The <u>salt</u> we put on <u>food</u> is a chemical called <u>SODIUM CHLORIDE</u>.

2) It is used to <u>PRESERVE</u> food (make it <u>last longer</u>). It is also used to <u>FLAVOUR</u> food (make it <u>taste nicer</u>).

3) It is mainly found in the <u>SEA</u> or <u>UNDERGROUND</u>.

4) The salt found <u>underground</u> is called a <u>salt DEPOSIT</u>.

5) There are <u>huge deposits</u> of salt under <u>Cheshire</u>.

6) You can get salt out of deposits by <u>NORMAL MINING</u> or <u>SOLUTION MINING</u>.

Normal Mining — Digging Out the Salt

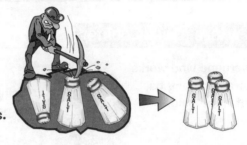

1) Salt is brought up to the surface as <u>ROCK SALT</u>.

2) Rock salt is a <u>MIXTURE</u> of <u>salt</u> and <u>other materials</u>.

3) The salt is then <u>SEPARATED</u> out from the other materials.

Solution Mining — Dissolving the Salt

1) <u>HOT WATER</u> is pumped underground.

2) This <u>DISSOLVES</u> the salt.

3) Then the <u>SALT SOLUTION</u> is <u>forced to the surface</u>.

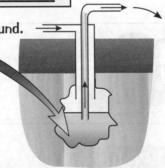

Mining can Cause Subsidence

1) Mining can leave large <u>HOLES</u> in the ground.

2) If they're not filled in, the land could <u>slide into the holes</u> — this is called <u>SUBSIDENCE</u>.

3) It makes the land <u>DANGEROUS</u> for <u>people</u> and <u>buildings</u>.

Practice Questions

1) Give <u>two places</u> salt can be found.

2) Describe how <u>solution mining</u> works.

3) Give <u>one problem</u> caused by <u>mining</u>.

Electrolysis

You can make stuff from salt using <u>electricity</u>.

Electrolysis of Brine Gives Chlorine, Hydrogen and Sodium Hydroxide

1) <u>Sodium chloride (SALT) solution</u> is called <u>BRINE</u>.

2) If you pass an <u>ELECTRIC CURRENT</u> through brine it <u>SPLITS UP</u>.

3) This is called <u>ELECTROLYSIS</u>.

4) Electrolysis of brine makes <u>chlorine</u>, <u>hydrogen</u> and <u>sodium hydroxide</u>.

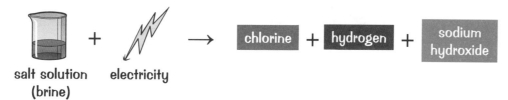

salt solution + electricity → chlorine + hydrogen + sodium hydroxide
(brine)

5) The bits that <u>conduct ELECTRICITY</u> in electrolysis are called <u>ELECTRODES</u>.

6) There are two of them — the <u>CATHODE</u> and the <u>ANODE</u>.

7) <u>Hydrogen</u> is made at the <u>cathode</u>.

8) <u>Chlorine</u> is made at the <u>anode</u>.

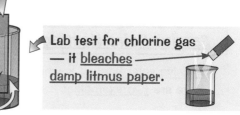

Lab test for chlorine gas
— it <u>bleaches</u>
damp litmus paper.

9) The <u>electrodes</u> are made of an <u>INERT</u> material — this just means that they <u>won't react</u>.

The Chemicals Made by Electrolysis are Really Useful

CHEMICAL	USES
CHLORINE	To <u>disinfectant water</u> Making <u>solvents</u> Making <u>plastics</u> (like <u>PVC</u>) Making <u>household bleach</u>
HYDROGEN	Making <u>margarine</u>
SODIUM HYDROXIDE	Making <u>soap</u> Making <u>household bleach</u>

Practice Questions

1) Name <u>three chemicals</u> that are made by the <u>electrolysis of brine</u>.

2) Give <u>one</u> use for <u>sodium hydroxide</u>.

Using the Sun's Energy

The Sun is very <u>hot</u> and very <u>bright</u>. This means it's giving out a lot of <u>energy</u>.

The Sun **can be used** for Heat **and** Electricity

Photocells

Photocells transfer <u>SUNLIGHT</u> into <u>ELECTRICITY</u>.

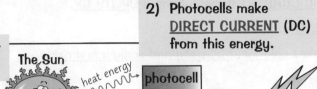

1) The Sun gives out <u>loads</u> of <u>energy</u>.

2) Photocells make <u>DIRECT CURRENT</u> (DC) from this energy.

3) Direct current is <u>electricity</u> that flows the <u>SAME WAY</u> all the time.

<u>Batteries</u> also make direct current.

The Sun

heat energy

light energy

photocell

DC electricity

4) The bigger the <u>SURFACE AREA</u> of the cell, the bigger the <u>POWER</u> or <u>CURRENT</u>.

Passive Solar Heating

<u>Passive solar heating</u> is when the Sun's radiation (energy) is <u>ABSORBED</u> by a <u>surface</u> and turned to <u>HEAT</u>. Here are <u>two examples</u>:

WINDOWS

glass

heat and light from sun

<u>Glass</u> lets <u>HEAT</u> and <u>LIGHT</u> into a building.

The cat inside <u>absorbs</u> it and <u>HEATS UP</u>.

SOLAR OVENS

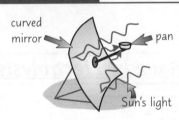

curved mirror

pan

Sun's light

<u>Curved</u> mirrors <u>focus</u> the Sun's light on to the pan.

The pan <u>absorbs</u> it and <u>HEATS UP</u>.

This can be used to <u>HEAT FOOD</u>.

Wind Power

The <u>Sun</u> makes <u>wind</u>, which can <u>drive (turn)</u> TURBINES to make <u>ELECTRICITY</u>.

1) The Sun heats the <u>air</u>, making it <u>rise</u>.

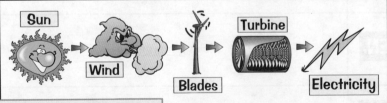

Sun

Wind

Blades

Turbine

Electricity

2) Cold air <u>rushes in</u> to take its place.

3) This is a <u>CONVECTION CURRENT</u> — we know it as <u>wind</u>.

4) Wind can be used to <u>DRIVE TURBINES</u>.

5) The turbines change the <u>kinetic energy</u> (movement) of the wind into <u>ELECTRICITY</u>.

This is done by turning a <u>generator</u> — see page 111.

Practice Questions

1) What type of electricity do <u>photocells</u> make, <u>AC</u> or <u>DC</u>?

2) Name one example of <u>passive solar heating</u>.

3) How does the <u>sun</u> make <u>wind</u>?

Using the Sun's Energy

Using energy from the Sun can have <u>bad points</u> as well as <u>good points</u>.

Photocells **and** Wind Power **Have** Good and Bad Points

	ADVANTAGES (<u>good</u> points)	DISADVANTAGES (<u>bad</u> points)
PHOTOCELLS 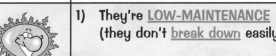	1) They're <u>LOW-MAINTENANCE</u> (they don't <u>break down</u> easily). 2) They <u>don't</u> need <u>FUEL</u>. 3) They <u>don't</u> need <u>POWER CABLES</u>. 4) They have a <u>LONG LIFE</u>. 5) They can be used in <u>REMOTE</u> (hard to reach) places. 6) Energy from the Sun is <u>RENEWABLE</u> (it won't run out). 7) They <u>don't</u> produce any <u>POLLUTING WASTE</u>.	Photocells <u>NEED SUNLIGHT</u>. So they <u>DON'T</u> make electricity at <u>NIGHT</u> or when the <u>WEATHER'S BAD</u>. 
WIND POWER	1) Energy from wind is <u>RENEWABLE</u> (it won't run out). 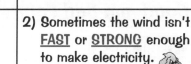 2) It doesn't produce any <u>POLLUTING WASTE</u>.	1) It can be hard to find enough <u>SPACE</u> in <u>windy places</u> to <u>build</u> wind turbines. 2) Sometimes the wind isn't <u>FAST</u> or <u>STRONG</u> enough to make electricity. 3) Turbines can <u>SPOIL THE VIEW</u> (<u>visual pollution</u>). 

Practice Questions

1) Is energy from the Sun <u>renewable</u> or <u>non-renewable</u>?
2) What is the main <u>disadvantage</u> of <u>photocells</u>?
3) Give one <u>advantage</u> of <u>wind power</u>.

Producing and Distributing Electricity

Most electricity is made in <u>power stations</u> and then sent out by the <u>National Grid</u>.

The National Grid Carries Electricity

The <u>NATIONAL GRID</u> is all the <u>power lines</u> that cover <u>the whole country</u>:

1) Electricity is <u>GENERATED</u> (made) in <u>power stations</u> from a <u>SOURCE OF ENERGY</u>.

For example, burning fuels is a source of energy.

2) The National Grid carries this electricity from <u>power stations</u>.

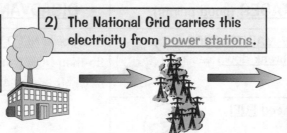

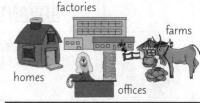

3) It's sent to <u>CONSUMERS ANYWHERE</u> in the country.

Most Power Stations Make Electricity From Steam

<u>Power stations</u> change energy into <u>electricity</u> like this:

1) <u>Heat</u> energy from a <u>FUEL</u> makes <u>STEAM</u> from water.

2) The <u>steam</u> turns a <u>TURBINE</u>.

3) The <u>turbine</u> turns a <u>GENERATOR</u>.

4) The <u>generator</u> makes <u>ELECTRICITY</u> from this movement (see next page).

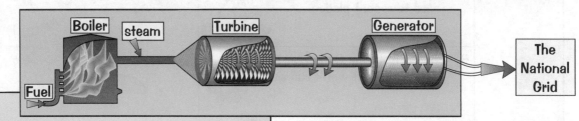

FUELS:
1) <u>FOSSIL</u> fuels — <u>coal</u>, <u>oil</u>, <u>natural gas</u>.
2) Renewable <u>BIOMASS</u> — <u>wood</u>, <u>straw</u>, <u>manure</u>.
3) <u>NUCLEAR</u> fuels — <u>uranium</u> and <u>plutonium</u>.

These two types are <u>burnt</u> in the boiler to make heat, but nuclear fuels aren't.

Fuels Have Good and Bad Points

FOSSIL FUELS

☺ They make a <u>LOT OF ENERGY</u>.

☺ The power stations are <u>EASY to set up</u>.

☹ Burning fossil fuels makes <u>carbon dioxide</u> (see p. 115) and other <u>pollution</u>.

☹ We have to <u>buy</u> them from <u>other countries</u>.

☹ They're <u>NON-RENEWABLE</u> — they'll <u>run out</u>.

BIOMASS

☹ It doesn't make <u>as much energy</u> as <u>fossil fuels</u>.

☹ <u>Forests</u> may be <u>cleared</u> to make room to grow it.

☺ It's '<u>CARBON NEUTRAL</u>' — it doesn't add to the <u>total</u> amount of <u>carbon dioxide</u> in the air.

☺ We don't need to <u>buy</u> it from other countries, so we <u>CONTROL</u> the <u>price</u> and <u>supply</u>.

☺ It's <u>RENEWABLE</u> — it won't run out.

Practice Questions
1) What is the <u>National Grid</u>?
2) Give one <u>bad point</u> about <u>fossil fuels</u>.

The Dynamo Effect

Electricity can be made using a <u>coil of wire</u> and a <u>magnet</u>. Handy.

The Dynamo Effect Makes Electricity

1) A <u>CURRENT</u> (flow) of <u>ELECTRICITY</u> can be made by...

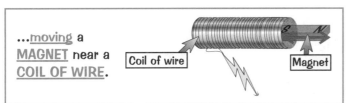

...<u>moving</u> a **MAGNET** near a <u>COIL OF WIRE</u>.

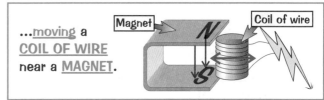

...<u>moving</u> a <u>COIL OF WIRE</u> near a <u>MAGNET</u>.

2) This is called the <u>DYNAMO EFFECT</u>.

3) To <u>INCREASE</u> the <u>current</u> you have to <u>INCREASE</u> the <u>DYNAMO EFFECT</u>.

4) You can do this by <u>INCREASING</u> at least one of these:

- THE STRENGTH OF THE MAGNET.
- THE NUMBER OF TURNS ON THE COIL.
- THE SPEED OF MOVEMENT.

Generators Use the Dynamo Effect

1) <u>GENERATORS</u> make electricity using the <u>dynamo effect</u>:

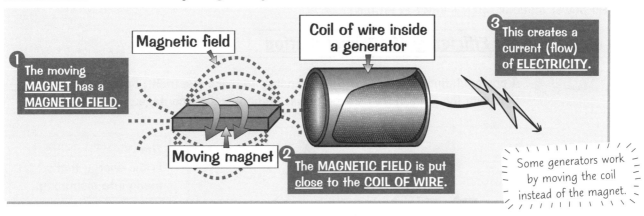

Magnetic field

Coil of wire inside a generator

① The moving **MAGNET** has a **MAGNETIC FIELD**.

Moving magnet

② The <u>MAGNETIC FIELD</u> is put <u>close</u> to the <u>COIL OF WIRE</u>.

③ This creates a current (flow) of <u>ELECTRICITY</u>.

Some generators work by moving the coil instead of the magnet.

2) Generators make an <u>ALTERNATING CURRENT</u> (AC). This is current that <u>CHANGES DIRECTION</u>.

3) This is different to <u>DIRECT CURRENT</u> (DC), which <u>batteries</u> make.

4) If you looked at AC on a <u>display</u>, you'd see something like this:

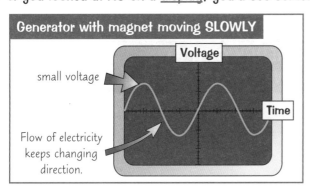

Generator with magnet moving SLOWLY

Voltage

small voltage

Time

Flow of electricity keeps changing direction.

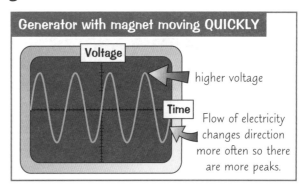

Generator with magnet moving QUICKLY

Voltage

higher voltage

Time

Flow of electricity changes direction more often so there are more peaks.

Practice Questions

1) Name <u>one</u> thing you can do to <u>increase</u> the <u>dynamo effect</u>.
2) What type of current do <u>generators</u> make, <u>AC</u> or <u>DC</u>?

Module P2 — Living for the Future

Supplying Electricity Efficiently

Sending electricity round the country is best done at a <u>high voltage</u>.

Electricity is Sent Around the Country at a High Voltage

1) Electricity can be <u>TRANSMITTED</u> (sent out) at <u>either</u> a <u>HIGH CURRENT</u> or a <u>HIGH VOLTAGE</u>.

HIGH CURRENT You <u>LOSE loads of ENERGY</u> as <u>HEAT</u> in the power lines. This wasted energy <u>COSTS MONEY</u>.

HIGH VOLTAGE The <u>CURRENT</u> is <u>LOW</u> so you <u>DON'T lose much ENERGY</u> as <u>HEAT</u> in the power lines.

wasted heat
HIGH CURRENT
high costs

2) So electricity is sent out at a <u>HIGH VOLTAGE</u> to <u>reduce</u> the <u>ENERGY WASTE</u> and <u>COSTS</u>.

3) <u>TRANSFORMERS</u> are used to <u>increase</u> or <u>decrease</u> the voltage.

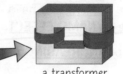
a transformer

Power Stations Waste Energy

1) A <u>LOT</u> of the energy put into a <u>power station</u> to make electricity is <u>WASTED</u>.

2) So power stations <u>AREN'T VERY EFFICIENT</u>.

Have a look back at page 57 for more stuff on efficiency.

Calculating the Efficiency of a Power Station

EXAMPLE A power station uses <u>500 000 J</u> of energy to make electricity but <u>wastes 300 000 J</u>. Calculate the <u>EFFICIENCY</u> of the power station as a percentage.

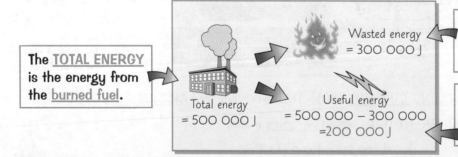

The <u>TOTAL ENERGY</u> is the energy from the <u>burned fuel</u>.

Wasted energy = 300 000 J

Total energy = 500 000 J

Useful energy = 500 000 – 300 000 = 200 000 J

The <u>WASTED ENERGY</u> is the energy that's <u>NOT</u> made into electricity.

The <u>USEFUL ENERGY</u> is the amount of <u>electricity</u> made. Useful = Total – Wasted

ANSWER You can use this equation to work out the <u>EFFICIENCY</u>:

$$\text{EFFICIENCY} = \frac{\text{USEFUL ENERGY OUTPUT}}{\text{TOTAL ENERGY INPUT}} \times 100$$

Page 6 will help you with equations.

$$\text{EFFICIENCY} = \frac{\text{USEFUL energy}}{\text{TOTAL energy}} \times 100 = \frac{200\ 000}{500\ 000} \times 100 = \underline{40\ \%}$$

Practice Questions

1) Is electricity sent around the country at a <u>high current</u> or a <u>high voltage</u>?

2) A power station uses <u>600 000 000 J</u> of energy to make <u>180 000 000 J</u> of electricity. Calculate the <u>efficiency</u> of the power station as a <u>percentage</u>.

Power

Electrical appliances have to be given <u>electrical energy</u> to do their job.

All Appliances have Power Ratings

1) Things that need electricity to work are called <u>APPLIANCES</u>.

2) All appliances have a <u>POWER RATING</u>.

3) The <u>power rating</u> tells you the <u>ENERGY</u> supplied <u>EVERY SECOND</u>.

A TV is an appliance.

electricity ➡ ➡ light, heat and sound

Energy supplied means how much electricity the thing needs to run.

UNITS

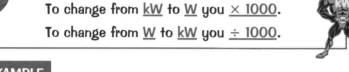

<u>POWER</u> is measured in <u>WATTS</u>, W, or <u>KILOWATTS</u>, kW.

<u>1 kW = 1000 W</u>.

To change from <u>kW</u> to <u>W</u> you × 1000.

To change from <u>W</u> to <u>kW</u> you ÷ 1000.

Energy is measured in joules, J.

EXAMPLE

<u>2000 J of energy</u> is supplied to this kettle <u>every second</u>.

2 kW

<u>100 J of energy</u> is supplied to this bulb <u>every second</u>.

100 W

• The kettle needs <u>more energy every second</u> than the bulb.

• The kettle has a <u>HIGHER POWER RATING</u> than the bulb.

Power is Voltage x Current

Use this equation to find the <u>power rating</u> of an appliance:

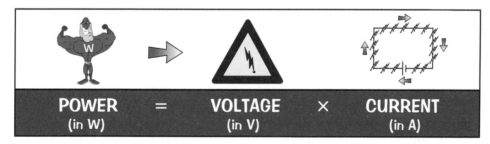

| POWER (in W) | = | VOLTAGE (in V) | × | CURRENT (in A) |

EXAMPLE:

A hair dryer is supplied with a voltage of <u>230 V</u> and a current of <u>4 A</u>. What is the <u>power rating</u> of the hair dryer in <u>kilowatts</u>?

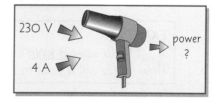
230 V
4 A
power ?

ANSWER:

Power = Voltage × Current = 230 V × 4 A = <u>920 W</u>

In kilowatts: 920 W ÷ 1000 = <u>0.92 kW</u>

Practice Questions

1) Is <u>power</u> measured in <u>watts</u> or <u>joules</u>?

2) A speaker has a voltage of <u>20 V</u> and a current of <u>5 A</u>. What is the <u>power rating</u> of the speaker?

Module P2 — Living for the Future

Power

Electricity costs money. You can work out how much it costs to use electrical appliances.

Kilowatt-hours are UNITS of Energy

1) The unit of electrical ENERGY SUPPLIED is the KILOWATT-HOUR (kWh).

2) You can find the energy supplied to an appliance using this equation:

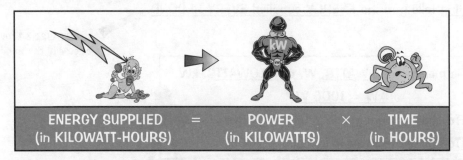

ENERGY SUPPLIED = POWER × TIME
(in KILOWATT-HOURS)   (in KILOWATTS)   (in HOURS)

EXAMPLE:
A tumble dryer has a power of 4 kW. It's on for 1.5 hours.
How much energy is supplied to it?

ANSWER:
Energy supplied = Power × Time = 4 kW × 1.5 h = 6 kWh

Electricity Costs Money

1) The COST of using an appliance depends on its POWER RATING and HOW LONG IT'S ON FOR.

HIGHER POWER RATING = HIGHER COST   LONGER TIME = HIGHER COST

2) You can work out the COST OF ENERGY SUPPLIED with this formula:

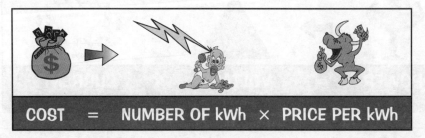

COST = NUMBER OF kWh × PRICE PER kWh

EXAMPLE:
A lightbulb uses 8 kWh in one month. 1 kWh costs 10p.
How much will it cost to use the lightbulb for one month?

ANSWER:
Cost = number of kWh × cost per kWh = 8 × 10p = 80p

Practice Questions

1) True or false: the unit of energy supplied to an appliance is the kilowatt-hour.
2) An iron uses 10 kWh in ten days. 1 kWh costs 10p. How much will it cost to use the iron for ten days?

The Greenhouse Effect

The atmosphere keeps us warm by trapping heat.

Some Radiation can Pass Through the Atmosphere

1) The Earth has a layer of gases around it called the ATMOSPHERE.

2) THE SUN gives out electromagnetic radiation.

Page 62 has more on electromagnetic (EM) radiation.

3) Most wavelengths of electromagnetic radiation PASS THROUGH the atmosphere.

4) Some wavelengths (such as infrared) are ABSORBED by the gases.

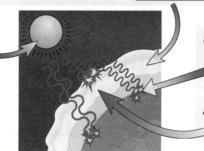

The Greenhouse Effect Helps to Keep the Earth Warm

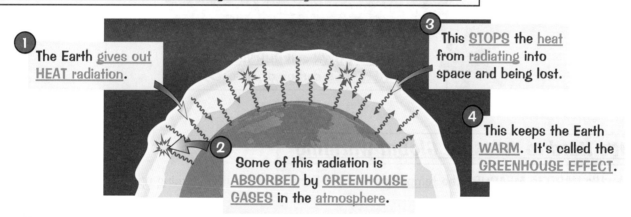

1 The Earth gives out HEAT radiation.

2 Some of this radiation is ABSORBED by GREENHOUSE GASES in the atmosphere.

3 This STOPS the heat from radiating into space and being lost.

4 This keeps the Earth WARM. It's called the GREENHOUSE EFFECT.

1) CARBON DIOXIDE, METHANE and WATER VAPOUR are three greenhouse gases.

2) They come from NATURAL and MAN-MADE sources:

GREENHOUSE GAS	NATURAL SOURCES	MAN-MADE SOURCES
CARBON DIOXIDE	Respiration (how plants and animals make energy) Volcanoes	Burning fossil fuels Chopping down and burning trees
METHANE	Volcanoes Wetlands Digestion in animals	Cattle farming Landfill waste (rubbish tips)
WATER VAPOUR	Oceans Rivers Seas Lakes	Power stations

Practice Questions

1) True or false: infrared radiation is not absorbed by the atmosphere.

2) Name three greenhouse gases.

Global Warming and Climate Change

We <u>need</u> the greenhouse effect to keep the Earth warm — just <u>not too much</u> of it.

The Earth's Temperature has Gone Up

1) Over the last 150 years, the <u>TEMPERATURE</u> of the Earth has gone <u>UP</u>.

2) This is called <u>GLOBAL WARMING</u>.

3) <u>Increased global warming</u> is causing <u>CLIMATE CHANGE</u> — the whole world's <u>weather</u> is <u>changing</u>.

4) There's a lot of <u>EVIDENCE</u> that <u>INCREASED CARBON DIOXIDE</u> has caused <u>global warming</u>.

5) So there are <u>THREE</u> main reasons for this climate change:

1. WE ARE RELEASING MORE CARBON DIOXIDE	2. WE ARE USING MORE ENERGY
Burning <u>FOSSIL FUELS</u> releases carbon dioxide.	We use <u>extra energy</u> today. This means we have to burn more <u>FOSSIL FUELS</u> that release carbon dioxide.

3. WE ARE CHOPPING DOWN MORE TREES

This is called <u>DEFORESTATION</u>.
<u>CHOPPING DOWN</u> and <u>BURNING</u> trees <u>RELEASES</u> carbon dioxide.

It's Hard to Measure Global Warming

1) It's <u>HARD</u> to <u>MEASURE</u> the <u>temperature</u> of the Earth to see if it's warming up.

Temperature changes can be <u>DIFFERENT</u> all over the world.

We're <u>NOT SURE</u> about the temperatures <u>more than 100 years ago</u>.

2) Scientists working on global warming <u>SHARE</u> their results.

3) This means scientists can <u>check</u> that their results <u>match</u> everyone else's.

Changes to the Weather can have Human and Natural Causes

<u>CHANGES</u> to the <u>WEATHER</u> can be caused <u>NATURALLY</u> or by <u>HUMAN</u> activities:

HUMAN ACTIVITIES

- <u>FACTORIES</u> make <u>DUST</u>.
- The dust can <u>reflect heat</u> from cities back down to Earth.
- This can cause <u>WARMING</u>.

NATURAL CAUSES

- <u>ASH</u> and <u>GASES</u> are thrown into the atmosphere by <u>VOLCANOES</u>.
- This can <u>reflect radiation</u> from the Sun <u>back into space</u>.
- This can cause the Earth to <u>COOL DOWN</u>.

Practice Questions

1) Give <u>one</u> reason for <u>climate change</u>.
2) Describe how <u>human activities</u> can cause <u>warming</u>.

Radioactive Materials

You hear a lot about <u>nuclear radiation</u> on the news. Here's a chance to learn more about it.

Uranium and Plutonium are Radioactive

1) <u>URANIUM</u> is a <u>non-renewable energy resource</u>.

2) It's used in <u>nuclear power stations</u> to make electricity.

3) <u>PLUTONIUM</u> is a <u>waste product</u> from nuclear power.

4) It can also be used to make <u>nuclear bombs</u>.

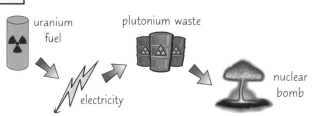

Getting Rid of Radioactive Waste is Difficult

1) Waste from nuclear power stations is <u>RADIOACTIVE</u>, so it's <u>harmful</u> (see below).

2) But it does <u>NOT</u> cause <u>global warming</u> like carbon dioxide does (see page 116).

3) Here's how to <u>DISPOSE</u> (get rid) of radioactive waste:

<u>LOW-LEVEL</u> (<u>not very</u> radioactive) waste can be <u>buried</u> in <u>LANDFILL</u> sites.

<u>MORE</u> radioactive waste can be sealed in <u>GLASS</u> and left <u>UNDERGROUND</u>.

Some radioactive waste can be <u>REPROCESSED</u> (recycled) into useful stuff.

There are Three Kinds of Nuclear Radiation

1) <u>Radioactive materials</u> give out <u>NUCLEAR RADIATION</u> over time.

2) There are <u>THREE</u> kinds of nuclear radiation:

3) They all cause <u>IONISATION</u>:

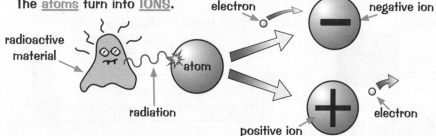

- <u>Ionisation</u> is when the radiation makes <u>atoms</u> <u>LOSE</u> or <u>GAIN</u> <u>ELECTRONS</u>.

- The <u>atoms</u> turn into <u>IONS</u>.

<u>NEGATIVE</u> ions are made when atoms <u>GAIN</u> electrons.

<u>POSITIVE</u> ions are made when atoms <u>LOSE</u> electrons.

4) <u>Ionisation</u> is <u>HARMFUL</u> because it can <u>DAMAGE CELLS</u> and cause <u>CANCER</u>.

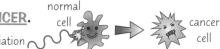

Practice Questions

1) Give <u>one way</u> of getting rid of <u>nuclear waste</u>.

2) Name the <u>three</u> kinds of <u>nuclear radiation</u>.

Nuclear Radiation

Alpha, beta and gamma radiation can do different things.

Radiation can Pass Through Materials

Different types of radiation can PASS FURTHER THROUGH some materials than others.

How penetrating it is just means how far it can pass through something.

ALPHA RADIATION: LEAST PENETRATING

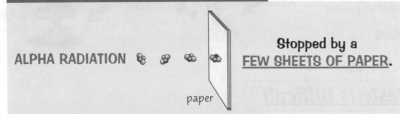

ALPHA RADIATION

paper

Stopped by a FEW SHEETS OF PAPER.

BETA RADIATION: A BIT PENETRATING

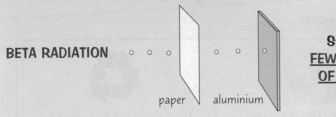

BETA RADIATION

paper   aluminium

Stopped by a FEW MILLIMETRES OF ALUMINIUM.

GAMMA RADIATION: MOST PENETRATING

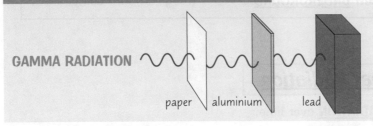

GAMMA RADIATION

paper   aluminium   lead

Mostly stopped by a FEW CENTIMETRES OF LEAD.

You Must Handle Radioactive Materials Safely

There are **FIVE** ways that you can **PROTECT** yourself from nuclear radiation:

1 Store radioactive materials in a LABELLED and SHIELDED (protected) box.

2 Handle radioactive materials with TONGS.

3 Keep radioactive materials as FAR from the body as possible.

4 Keep your EXPOSURE TIME SHORT. This means spending as little time as you can around radioactive materials.

5 Wear PROTECTIVE CLOTHING.

Practice Questions

1) Which is the most penetrating: alpha, beta or gamma radiation?
2) Give one way that you can protect yourself from nuclear radiation.

Uses of Nuclear Radiation

Nuclear radiation can be very <u>dangerous</u>. But it can be very <u>useful</u> too.

Alpha Radiation — Smoke Detectors

<u>SMOKE DETECTORS</u> have a <u>RADIOACTIVE</u> material inside them.

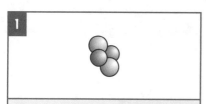

1 The radioactive material gives out <u>ALPHA RADIATION</u>.

2 If there's a fire the <u>smoke</u> takes in the <u>alpha radiation</u>.

3 This makes the <u>ALARM</u> go off.

Beta Radiation — Tracers and Measuring Thickness

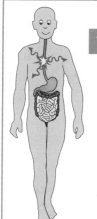

TRACERS

Things that give off <u>beta radiation</u> can be used as <u>TRACERS</u> in <u>MEDICINE</u>.

Tracers show if the body's <u>WORKING PROPERLY</u>.

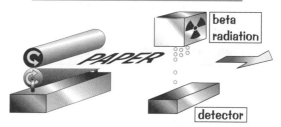

MEASURING PAPER THICKNESS

You can measure <u>HOW THICK</u> paper is by measuring much <u>beta radiation</u> it <u>STOPS</u>.

Factories that <u>make paper</u> use it to make sure their paper is the <u>RIGHT THICKNESS</u>.

Gamma Radiation — Hospitals and Industry

There are lots of uses of <u>gamma radiation</u>. For example:

gamma ray

cancer cell

<u>TREATING CANCERS</u>

Things that <u>give off</u> gamma radiation can be used as <u>TRACERS</u>.

<u>STERILISING</u> medical <u>instruments</u> — getting rid of all the harmful germs.

<u>NON-DESTRUCTIVE TESTING</u> — testing something without taking it apart.

Practice Questions

1) Give <u>one use</u> of <u>alpha radiation</u>.
2) Give <u>one use</u> of <u>beta radiation</u>.
3) Give <u>one use</u> of <u>gamma radiation</u>.

The Solar System and the Universe

Ooooh... <u>Space</u> stuff. Cool.

Planets Orbit the Sun

1) The <u>SOLAR SYSTEM</u> looks a bit like this:

The <u>SUN</u> is in the <u>middle</u>.

All the other stuff like <u>planets</u> ORBIT (go round) it.

The <u>EARTH</u> is the <u>third</u> planet from the Sun.

The <u>ASTEROID BELT</u> (p. 121) comes between <u>Mars</u> and <u>Jupiter</u>.

2) You need to learn the <u>ORDER</u> of the planets:

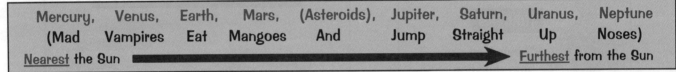

Mercury,	Venus,	Earth,	Mars,	(Asteroids),	Jupiter,	Saturn,	Uranus,	Neptune
(Mad	Vampires	Eat	Mangoes	And	Jump	Straight	Up	Noses)

<u>Nearest</u> the Sun ———————————————————————→ <u>Furthest</u> from the Sun

The Sun is a Star

1) Our <u>SUN</u> is one <u>STAR</u> in the <u>Universe</u>.

2) Stars are much <u>BIGGER</u> than <u>planets</u>.

3) They all <u>GIVE OUT</u> lots of their own <u>LIGHT</u>.

4) This is why you can <u>SEE</u> them, even though they're <u>far away</u>.

Stars give off light because they are hot.   light

The Universe Contains Everything

As well as <u>stars</u> and <u>planets</u>, these things are found in the <u>Universe</u> too:

COMETS	METEORS	GALAXIES	BLACK HOLES
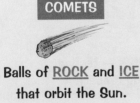	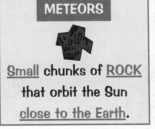		
Balls of <u>ROCK</u> and <u>ICE</u> that orbit the Sun. They are <u>SMALLER</u> than planets.	<u>Small</u> chunks of <u>ROCK</u> that orbit the Sun <u>close to the Earth</u>.	<u>LARGE GROUPS</u> of stars.	<u>GRAVITY</u> pulls <u>everything</u> in the Universe towards <u>everything else</u>. The gravity of a <u>black hole</u> is so <u>HUGE</u> that <u>not even light can ESCAPE</u> from it.

Practice Questions

1) True or false: the <u>Sun</u> is a <u>meteor</u>.

2) Put these things in <u>order</u> from <u>smallest</u> to <u>largest</u>: star, planet, comet, galaxy.

Asteroids and Comets

The stuff in the Solar System is mostly just <u>rocks</u> and <u>gases</u>.

Asteroids are Rocks

1) When the Solar System was made, the <u>rocks</u> between Mars and Jupiter <u>didn't form a planet</u>.

2) These <u>leftover</u> lumps of <u>rock</u> are called <u>ASTEROIDS</u>.

Asteroids Can Crash into Planets

1) In the past <u>asteroids</u> have <u>HIT EARTH</u>.

2) This can cause <u>problems</u>:

They can start <u>FIRES</u>.

They can make big <u>CRATERS</u> (holes) in the ground.

They <u>eject</u> (throw out) loads of <u>HOT ROCKS</u> and <u>DUST</u> into the air.

This means that types of plant or animal don't exist anymore.

The <u>dust</u> that's thrown out can <u>BLOCK OUT</u> the <u>sunlight</u>.

This can cause <u>CLIMATE CHANGE</u>.

Climate change can cause <u>species</u> to become <u>EXTINCT</u>.

3) There's <u>EVIDENCE</u> that asteroids have hit Earth in the <u>past</u>:

- <u>BIG CRATERS</u>.
- <u>ELEMENTS</u> that <u>aren't normally</u> found on the <u>Earth</u> have been found in <u>ROCKS</u>.
- <u>Sudden changes</u> in <u>fossil numbers</u> between different <u>layers</u> of rock.

← This species died out very quickly:

It's not in these layers.

It's in this older layer.

Comets are Made From Ice and Dust

<u>COMETS</u> come from objects orbiting the Sun <u>FAR BEYOND</u> the planets.

They leave a bright <u>tail</u> of <u>debris</u> (dust and ice) behind them.

They are made of <u>DUST</u> and <u>ICE</u>.

COMET

They have <u>HIGHLY ELLIPTICAL</u> orbits (like squashed circles).

STAR

Comets <u>SPEED UP</u> as they get <u>NEARER</u> to stars (like the Sun).

Practice Questions

1) The <u>asteroids</u> in our Solar System are found <u>between two planets</u>. Name the two <u>planets</u>.

2) What are <u>comets</u> made from?

NEOs and the Moon

There are loads of lumps of rock just <u>whizzing about</u> in space. One of them might be coming <u>straight at you</u>.

NEOs Could Hit Earth

1) <u>NEAR-EARTH OBJECTS</u> (NEOs) are <u>ASTEROIDS</u> or <u>COMETS</u> that could <u>HIT</u> the Earth.

2) They are on a possible <u>COLLISION COURSE</u> with Earth.

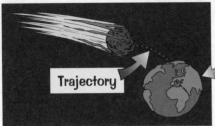

3) Scientists use <u>powerful TELESCOPES</u> and <u>SATELLITES</u> to look for NEOs.

4) When they find one, they can work out its <u>TRAJECTORY</u> (the <u>path</u> it's going to take).

5) They use this to find out if it's going to <u>HIT US</u>.

6) NEOs can be <u>difficult to spot</u> because they're <u>SMALL</u> and <u>DARK</u>.

The Moon is Made From Left Over Rock

Scientists think that the <u>Moon</u> is <u>left over rock</u> from a <u>planet hitting the Earth</u>:

The <u>core</u> (centre) of the Earth is made from <u>iron</u>.

1 Billions of years ago a <u>smaller</u> planet <u>CRASHED INTO THE EARTH</u>.

2 The <u>IRON CORES</u> of the two planets <u>MERGED</u> (joined up) to form the Earth's core.

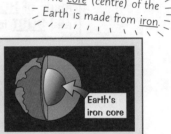

<u>Dense</u> materials are really <u>heavy</u> for their size.

4 This <u>dust</u> and <u>rock</u> came together to form the <u>MOON</u>. The Moon now <u>orbits</u> the Earth.

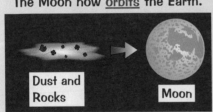

3

The <u>less dense</u> material was <u>THROWN OUT</u> as <u>DUST</u> and <u>ROCKS</u>.

We Measure Distances in Space Using Light Years

1) Space is <u>REALLY, REALLY BIG</u>.

2) We use <u>LIGHT YEARS</u> to measure <u>distances</u> in space:

> ONE LIGHT YEAR IS THE <u>DISTANCE LIGHT TRAVELS</u> IN <u>ONE YEAR</u>.

Practice Questions

1) What are <u>near-Earth objects</u>?

2) What is a <u>light year</u>?

Understanding the Universe

To <u>understand</u> the Universe we need to <u>explore</u> it by sending <u>someone</u> or <u>something</u> up there to look around.

We Can Explore Space Using Spacecraft

1) The Solar System is <u>big</u> — even <u>radio signals</u> take <u>hours</u> to cross it.

2) This means it takes a <u>long time</u> to <u>TRAVEL</u> anywhere in space.

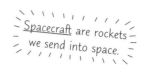

Spacecraft are rockets we send into space.

3) We can send up <u>SPACECRAFT</u> <u>with</u> or <u>without people</u> inside:

MANNED SPACECRAFT — DIFFICULT

<u>MANNED</u> spacecraft have <u>people</u> in to explore space.

The spacecraft needs to carry a lot of <u>FOOD</u>, <u>WATER</u> and <u>OXYGEN</u>.

It's <u>DIFFICULT</u> to keep the people <u>ALIVE</u> and <u>HEALTHY</u> for all that time.

UNMANNED SPACECRAFT — EASIER

1) <u>UNMANNED</u> spacecraft <u>don't</u> carry people.

2) So they <u>DON'T</u> have to carry <u>FOOD</u>, <u>WATER</u> and <u>OXYGEN</u>.

3) And they can cope with <u>conditions</u> that would be <u>LETHAL</u> (deadly) to humans.

- Unmanned spacecraft have <u>instruments</u> to send <u>INFORMATION</u> back to Earth.
- Spacecraft sent to places <u>NEAR Earth</u> can <u>bring back SAMPLES</u>.
- Spacecraft sent to really <u>FAR AWAY</u> planets have to <u>SEND DATA</u> (information) back.

information

The Universe Started with a Big Bang

BIG BANG THEORY

- At the start of time, <u>everything</u> in the Universe was <u>SQUASHED</u> into a <u>TINY SPACE</u>.
- Then it <u>exploded</u> in a <u>BIG BANG</u>.
- Then it started <u>EXPANDING</u> (spreading out) and <u>hasn't stopped</u> yet.

Before | After

THE EVIDENCE

- <u>MICROWAVE RADIATION</u> (see p. 66) can be picked up from <u>ALL PARTS</u> of the Universe.
- Scientists think this is <u>LEFT OVER</u> from the <u>Big Bang</u>.

- Most <u>GALAXIES</u> are <u>moving AWAY from us</u>.
- Galaxies that are <u>FURTHER away</u> are moving away <u>FASTER</u>.
- This shows that the Universe started with an <u>EXPLOSION</u>.

Practice Questions

1) Which spacecraft <u>doesn't</u> have to carry food, water and oxygen, <u>manned</u> or <u>unmanned</u>?

2) Describe the <u>Big Bang theory</u>.

The Life Cycle of Stars

Stars go through lots of STAGES in their lives. But they don't last forever — they have a FINITE LIFE.

Clouds of DUST and GAS

1 Stars start off as HUGE GAS CLOUDS.

BIG Star

2 They can grow into DIFFERENT SIZED stars...

SMALL Star

3 At the end of their life, big stars grow into RED SUPERGIANTS.

3 At the end of their life, small stars grow into RED GIANTS.

RED SUPERGIANT

RED GIANT

These stars are red because the surface COOLS.

4
- The star gets UNSTABLE.
- It throws off a layer of dust and gas.
- This layer is now called a PLANETARY NEBULA.

4 Eventually, they explode in a SUPERNOVA.

PLANETARY NEBULA

SUPERNOVA

5
- A hot, small and heavy solid core is left.
- This is called a WHITE DWARF.

NEUTRON STAR...

5
- The supernova throws a layer of dust and gas into space.
- This leaves a core called a NEUTRON STAR.

and a WHITE DWARF

...or BLACK HOLE

6 If the star is big enough it will become a BLACK HOLE.

Practice Questions

1) Red supergiants explode. What is this explosion called?
2) What is the last stage in the life cycle of a small star called?

Galileo and Copernicus

Scientists <u>change</u> their ideas as they <u>learn more</u> about the <u>Universe</u>.

We Used to Think the Universe Looked Different

1) A <u>MODEL</u> is an idea that explains something.

2) Our <u>models</u> of the <u>SIZE</u> and <u>SHAPE</u> of the Universe have <u>CHANGED</u> over time.

MODEL	DESCRIPTION
PTOLEMAIC	• This model was believed until the <u>1500s</u>. • The Sun, Moon, planets and stars all <u>orbit the EARTH</u>. • All their orbits are perfect <u>CIRCLES</u>. • The <u>Earth</u> is at the <u>CENTRE</u> of the Universe.
COPERNICAN	• This model was thought of in <u>1543</u>. • The Earth and planets all <u>orbit the SUN</u>. • The planets orbit in <u>CIRCLES</u>. • The <u>Sun</u> is the <u>CENTRE</u> of the Universe.
MODERN DAY	• This is what we think the Universe is like <u>today</u>. • The Earth and planets all <u>orbit the SUN</u>. • The planet's orbits are <u>NOT PERFECT CIRCLES</u>. • The Sun is <u>NOT AT THE CENTRE</u> of the universe.

Galileo Found Evidence for the Copernican Model

1) <u>GALILEO</u> was one of the first people to use a <u>TELESCOPE</u>.

2) He used it to find <u>EVIDENCE</u> for the <u>Copernican model</u>.

3) Models often <u>CHANGE</u> because of <u>TECHNOLOGICAL ADVANCES</u> (new technology).

GALILEO'S EVIDENCE

• Galileo saw <u>moons ORBITING JUPITER</u>.

• This showed <u>NOT EVERYTHING</u> orbits the Earth.

• So the Ptolemaic model was <u>WRONG</u>.

• Galileo saw <u>BIG CHANGES</u> in how <u>VENUS</u> looked from Earth.

• These changes could only be explained if Venus orbited <u>the Sun</u>.

• So this was <u>evidence</u> for the <u>Copernican</u> model.

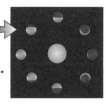

Practice Questions

1) What does <u>everything</u> orbit in the <u>Ptolemaic model</u>?

2) What <u>technology</u> was <u>Galileo</u> one of the first people to use?

3) What did <u>Galileo</u> see that proved the <u>Ptolemaic</u> model was <u>wrong</u>?

Answers

Module B1 — Understanding Ourselves

Page 7 — Fitness and Blood Pressure

1) false — Being healthy means you don't have a disease. Being fit means you find physical activity easy.
2) Any two from: smoking / being overweight / too much alcohol / stress

Page 8 — High Blood Pressure and Heart Disease

1) carbon monoxide, nicotine
2) saturated fat, salt

Page 9 — Eating Healthily

1) Any three from: carbohydrates, fats, proteins, fibre, vitamins, minerals, water
2) Because they're still growing.
3) any foods from animals

Page 10 — Diet Problems

1) Any one from: there are too many people and not enough food. / There isn't a lot of money to spend on farming.
2) Any one from: too much food / not enough exercise

Page 11 — Infectious Disease

1) true
2) They carry a disease without getting it themselves.

Page 12 — More On Infectious Disease

1) Any two from: skin / hydrochloric acid in the stomach / blood clots / sticky mucus in the airways
2) white blood cells

Page 13 — Cancer and Drug Development

1) bacteria
2) To make sure they're safe. To make sure they work.

Page 14 — Drugs: Use and Harm

1) They make the brain work faster.
2) false — Class A drugs are the most dangerous drugs.

Page 15 — Alcohol

1) Any three from: blurred vision / slurred speech / bad judgement / bad muscle control / lots of blood flow to the skin / sleepiness / rubbish balance
2) false — Doctors say men shouldn't drink more than 21 units of alcohol a week.
3) Because your reaction time is slower when you drink.

Page 16 — Smoking

1) carbon monoxide, nicotine, particulates, tar
2) carcinogens
3) Any three from: heart disease / cancer of the lung/throat/ mouth/oesophagus / bronchitis / emphysema / smoker's cough

Page 17 — The Eye

1) controls how much light gets through the pupil
2) optic nerve
3) cornea, lens

Page 18 — Vision

1) tell how far away something is / judge distances
2) special receptors in the retina are missing

Page 19 — Neurones

1) an electrical signal
2) the brain and the spinal cord

Page 20 — Reflexes

1) It's an action that stops you from hurting yourself.
2) They happen without you having to think about them.
3) false — Reflexes are fast.

Page 21 — Homeostasis

1) water content, body temperature, carbon dioxide level
2) sweats, more blood flows near the surface of the skin
3) Any one from: clinical thermometers / temperature-sensitive strips / digital thermometers / thermal imaging

Page 22 — Hormones and Controlling Blood Sugar

1) insulin
2) in the blood

Page 23 — Plant Hormones and Growth

1) plant growth hormones
2) true

Page 24 — Commercial Uses of Plant Hormones

1) plant growth hormones that only affect weeds
2) true
3) by adding plant hormones

Page 25 — Genes and Chromosomes

1) the nucleus
2) 23
3) different characteristics

Page 26 — Genes and the Environment

1) different versions of the same gene
2) Any one from: intelligence / body mass / height

Page 27 — Gametes and Genetic Variation

1) 23
2) when the sperm and the egg join to form a new cell

Page 28 — Genetic Disorders and Sex Inheritance

1) A genetic disorder where the body makes a lot of thick, sticky mucus in the airways and pancreas.
2) Any one from: How will I cope? / Should I have children? / Do I still want my baby?
3) a) XX
   b) XY

Module C1 — Carbon Chemistry

Page 29 — Atoms, Molecules and Compounds

1) negative
2) atoms joined together
3) a covalent bond

Page 30 — Chemical Formulas

1) 1
2) C_2H_6
3) 2 (writing Mg(OH)$_2$ is like writing MgOHOH)

Answers

Page 31 — Chemical Equations

1) hydrogen and oxygen
2) no (there are two oxygen atoms on the left and only one on the right)
3) yes

Page 32 — Food Additives

1) The hydrophobic part likes oil.
2) food colours, flavour enhancers
3) They stop food reacting with oxygen and going off.

Page 33 — Cooking and Chemical Change

1) denaturing
2) carbon dioxide

Page 34 — Perfumes

1) synthetic
2) They would wash off.
3) ester

Page 35 — Solutions

1) Any two from: water / esters (or ethyl acetate) / nail varnish remover (or acetone).
2) Something that's insoluble won't dissolve.
3) a solution

Page 36 — Paints and Pigments

1) it dries
2) the binding medium
3) It gives the paint its colour.

Page 37 — Special Pigments

1) it changes colour
2) they glow in the dark

Page 38 — Polymers

1) high pressure
2) styrene
3) Lots of small monomers join together.

Page 39 — Polymers and Their Uses

1) yes
2) no
3) You will get wet.

Page 40 — Getting Rid of Polymers

1) burying waste
2) biodegradable
3) It makes poisonous gases, it's a waste of plastic.

Page 41 — Hydrocarbons — Alkanes

1) single covalent bonds
2) no (it has a Cl in it)
3) yes

Page 42 — Hydrocarbons — Alkenes

1) hydrogen and carbon
2) yes
3) an alkene

Page 43 — Fractional Distillation of Crude Oil

1) It is made slowly or not made any more.
2) a fraction
3) The bottom end is the hottest.

Page 44 — Cracking

1) smaller alkanes and alkenes
2) Any two from: heat / a Bunsen burner and a catalyst / porcelain chips (Also accept: mineral wool / boiling tube / delivery tube / glass jar / water.)
3) Supply is how much of something there is. Demand is how much of something people want.

Page 45 — Use of Fossil Fuels

1) It damages their feathers. This can kill them.
2) Any four from: energy value / availability / pollution / cost / toxicity / storage / how easy it is to use

Page 46 — Burning Fuels

1) complete combustion
2) incomplete combustion

Page 47 — The Atmosphere

1) no
2) Photosynthesis adds oxygen.
3) nitrogen and oxygen

Page 48 — The Carbon Cycle

1) by photosynthesis
2) respiration and combustion
3) true

Page 49 — Air Pollution and Acid Rain

1) sulfur dioxide and oxides of nitrogen
2) carbon monoxide
3) Any two from: it kills trees / it kills plants and animals in rivers and lakes / it damages stone buildings and statues / it makes metals wear away or corrode.

Module P1 — Energy for the Home

Page 50 — Heat

1) They move around faster.
2) true
3) different temperatures

Page 51 — Specific Heat Capacity

1) Its mass, what it's made of and how much you want the temperature to rise (the temperature change).
2) Energy = mass × specific heat capacity × temperature change
   = 3 kg × 4200 J/Kg°C × 50 °C = 630 000 J

Page 52 — Melting and Boiling

1) Its temperature stays the same.
2) Energy = mass × specific latent heat
   = 5 kg × 334 000 J/kg = 1 670 000 J

Page 53 — Conduction and Convection

1) false — In solids, heat flows by conduction.
2) By stopping the liquid or gas moving.

Page 54 — Heat Radiation

1) true
2) The shiny foil reflects the heat back onto the bottom of the food to cook it more evenly.

Answers

Page 55 — Saving Energy

1) true
2) Insulating your house and buying more efficient sources and sinks.
3) Payback time = initial cost ÷ annual saving
   = £3000 ÷ £100 = 30 years

Page 56 — Saving Energy

1) Any one from: fibreglass / mineral wool / rock wool
2) It stops heat loss by radiation. The heat is reflected back into the room.
3) It stops the hot air going out. This reduces convection.

Page 57 — Efficiency

1) false — Efficient appliances don't waste much energy.
2) a) Useful energy = total energy − wasted energy
   = 300 000 J − 30 000 J = 270 000 J
   b) Efficiency = useful energy ÷ total energy × 100
   = 270 000 J ÷ 300 000 J × 100 = 90 %

Page 58 — Sankey Diagrams

1) How much energy that goes into an appliance is turned into useful energy and wasted energy.
2) false — Appliances that aren't efficient have thick wasted energy arrows.

Page 59 — Wave Basics

1) The distance from the rest position to a crest or trough.
2) Speed = frequency × wavelength = 3 Hz × 0.5 m = 1.5 m/s

Page 60 — Wave Properties — Reflection

1) true
2) angle of the ray bouncing off

Page 61 — Diffraction and Refraction

1) true
2) When a wave changes speed and direction as it passes from one substance to another.

Page 62 — EM Waves and Communication

1) infrared
2) Any one from: visible light / infrared
3) microwaves

Page 63 — Communicating with Light and Lasers

1) Morse code
2) false — Monochromatic light is all one colour.
3) Any one from: surgery / cutting tools in industry / 'sights' on weapons / laser light shows / dental treatments.

Page 64 — Infrared

1) Any two from: sending information short distances / remote controls / optical fibres / security systems / thermal imaging cameras / automatic doors
2) They work by flashing infrared light in different patterns. The pattern acts as a code. This code tells the electronic equipment what to do.

Page 65 — Optical Fibres

1) false — If a ray hits a boundary at an angle bigger than the critical angle, you get total internal reflection.
2) pulses of visible light

Page 66 — Microwaves

1) Any one from: if there's an obstacle in between you and the mobile phone mast. / If you're near a lake. / If the weather is wet.
2) true

Page 67 — Wireless Communication

1) Any one from: mobile phones / TVs / laptop computers / radios
2) Any one from: some areas can't pick up DAB at the moment. / The sound quality of DAB is often not as good as an FM radio broadcast.

Page 68 — Analogue and Digital Signals

1) analogue
2) false — All signals pick up noise when they travel long distances.
3) Because it is easier to remove noise from digital signals.

Page 69 — Ultraviolet Radiation

1) Any two from: sunburn / skin cancer / premature skin ageing / cataracts
2) true

Page 70 — UV and the Ozone Layer

1) Through the news and advertising.
2) A layer of gas around the Earth.
3) false — The fall in the amount of ozone was unexpected.

Page 71 — Seismic Waves

1) P-waves and S-waves
2) P-waves

Module B2 — Understanding Our Environment

Page 72 — Classification

1) Because some organisms fit into more than one group.
2) Any two from: they are multicellular. / They have cell walls made of cellulose. / They use energy from the sun to make their own food by photosynthesis.

Page 73 — More On Classification

1) They have six legs. Their bodies have three parts.
2) how organisms are related

Page 74 — Species

1) A group of organisms which can interbreed to produce fertile offspring.
2) because they live in different habitats

Page 75 — Food Chains and Food Webs

1) living things that make their own food
2) a stage in a food chain

Page 76 — Pyramids of Biomass and Numbers

1) how much all the organisms would weigh if you dried them out
2) false — Pyramids of numbers are nearly always pyramid-shaped.

Page 77 — Energy Transfer and Energy Flow

1) the Sun
2) Any two from: as heat from respiration / as waste products from excretion / as undigested food from egestion

Answers

Page 78 — Interactions Between Organisms

1) shelter, food, water
2) Any one from: tapeworms live in the stomachs of animals. They get food from the host, which can make the host ill. / Fleas get blood from dogs. Dogs just get bitten.

Page 79 — Predators and Prey

1) It's an animal that hunts and eats other animals.
2) false — Populations of predator and prey do affect each other.

Page 80 — Adaptations of Predators and Prey

1) Features that help organisms to compete and survive.
2) It makes it harder for predators to see prey.

Page 81 — Adaptations to Dry Environments

1) false — Organisms that are adapted to their environment are more likely to survive.
2) Any one from: a thick waxy layer. This is called a cuticle. It seals water in. / A thick stem. It stores water for when there's not much around. / Spines. These lose less water than leaves. / Long roots. This means they can get as much water as possible.
3) Any one from: they don't have sweat glands. This means they can't lose water by sweating. / They spend lots of time underground, where there's more water. / They make urine with very little water in it. This means they only lose a little water when they wee.

Page 82 — Adaptations to Hot and Cold Environments

1) Any one from: thick fur / a layer of blubber / small surface area / hibernate in winter / migrate to warmer places in winter
2) Any one from: large surface area / spend the day underground / have baths

Page 83 — Evolution and Natural Selection

1) true
2) Charles Darwin

Page 84 — The Carbon Cycle

1) carbon dioxide in the air
2) when animals eat the plants

Page 85 — The Nitrogen Cycle and Decomposition

1) So they can make proteins. They use the proteins to grow.
2) from nitrates in the soil

Page 86 — Human Impact on the Environment

1) fossil fuels, minerals
2) acid rain

Page 87 — Human Impact on the Environment

1) lichen
2) polluted water
3) false — You can also measure pollution directly.

Page 88 — Endangered Species

1) There are none of a species left alive.
2) It's hard to find resources like food and shelter if there aren't enough habitats.
3) true

Page 89 — Protecting Endangered Species

1) It can increase an endangered species' numbers.
2) false — Species are protected because they're important to a people's culture.

Page 90 — Sustainable Development

1) Providing for the needs of today's increasing population without harming the environment.
2) by using fishing quotas
3) to make meat / oil / cosmetics (make up) that can be sold

Module C2 — Chemical Resources

Page 91 — The Earth's Structure

1) lithosphere
2) seismic

Page 92 — Tectonic Plates

1) about 2.5 cm per year
2) evidence

Page 93 — Volcanoes

1) lava
2) Because ash from volcanoes makes the soil great for farming.
3) small

Page 94 — Limestone and Marble

1) granite
2) false — calcium carbonate → calcium oxide + carbon dioxide
3) Any two from: mining makes dust and a lot of noise. / It uses up land and destroys wildlife. / Moving rock can cause noise and pollution. / It costs money to make mines look pretty again.

Page 95 — Construction Materials

1) ores (rocks with metal in)
2) heat up sand
3) sand, water and gravel/aggregate

Page 96 — Extracting Pure Copper

1) reduction
2) Any two from: it stops copper running out so fast. / Uses less energy. / Saves fossil fuels so you make less pollution.

Page 97 — Alloys

1) An alloy is a mixture of two or more metals. Or it can be a mixture of a metal and a non-metal.
2) Lead and tin. To join electrical wires together.

Page 98 — Iron and Aluminium

1) Iron is more dense than aluminium.
2) hydrated iron (III) oxide (rust)

Page 99 — Building Cars

1) A car made out of steel would be cheaper than the same one made out of aluminium.
2) Any two from: it saves natural resources. / It saves money. / It means landfills are used less.

Page 100 — Acids and Bases

1) red
2) a salt and water

Page 101 — Reactions of Acids

1) a salt, water and carbon dioxide
2) calcium sulfate

Page 102 — Fertilisers

1) In any order: nitrogen, phosphorus and potassium.
2) If we use too much fertiliser it could pollute our water supplies. / If we use too much fertiliser it could cause eutrophication.

Answers

Page 103 — Making Fertilisers

1) nitrogen
2) ammonia

Page 104 — The Haber Process

1) the air
2) $N_2 + 3H_2 \rightleftharpoons 2NH_3$

Page 105 — The Cost of Production

1) more
2) A catalyst will speed up a reaction.
3) The materials used to make a product.

Page 106 — Salt

1) in the sea or underground
2) Hot water is pumped underground. This dissolves the salt. Then the salt solution is forced to the surface.
3) subsidence

Page 107 — Electrolysis

1) In any order: chlorine, sodium hydroxide and hydrogen
2) Any one from: making household bleach / making soap

Module P2 — Living for the Future

Page 108 — Using the Sun's Energy

1) DC
2) Any one from: windows / solar ovens
3) The Sun heats the air, making it rise. Cold air rushes in to take its place. This is a convection current — or wind.

Page 109 — Using the Sun's Energy

1) renewable
2) They need sunlight so don't make electricity at night or when the weather is bad.
3) Any one from: it will never run out/it's renewable / it doesn't produce any polluting waste.

Page 110 — Producing and Distributing Electricity

1) All the power lines that cover the whole country.
2) Any one from: burning them makes carbon dioxide and other pollution. / We have to buy them from other countries. / They're non-renewable — they'll run out.

Page 111 — The Dynamo Effect

1) Any one from: increase the strength of the magnet / increase the number of turns on the coil / increase the speed of movement.
2) AC

Page 112 — Supplying Electricity Efficiently

1) high voltage
2) efficiency = useful energy ÷ total energy × 100
   = 180 000 000 J ÷ 600 000 000 J × 100
   = 30 %

Page 113 — Power

1) watts
2) power = voltage × current
   = 20 V × 5 A
   = 100 W

Page 114 — Power

1) true
2) cost = number of kWh × price per kWh
   = 10 kWh × 10p
   = 100p (= £1)

Page 115 — The Greenhouse Effect

1) false — Infrared radiation is absorbed by the atmosphere.
2) Carbon dioxide, methane and water vapour.

Page 116 — Global Warming and Climate Change

1) Any one from: we are releasing more carbon dioxide / we are using more energy / we are chopping down more trees (deforestation).
2) Factories make dust. The dust can reflect heat from cities back down to Earth. This can cause warming.

Page 117 — Radioactive Materials

1) Any one from: low-level waste can be buried in landfill sites. / More radioactive waste can be sealed in glass and left underground. / Some radioactive waste can be reprocessed (recycled) into useful stuff.
2) alpha, beta and gamma

Page 118 — Nuclear Radiation

1) gamma
2) Any one from: store radioactive materials in a labelled and shielded box. / Keep your exposure time as short as possible. / Keep radioactive materials as far from the body as possible. / Handle radioactive materials with tongs. / Wear protective clothing.

Page 119 — Uses of Nuclear Radiation

1) smoke detectors
2) Any one from: tracers / measuring the thickness of paper
3) Any one from: treating cancers / tracers / sterilising medical instruments / non-destructive testing

Page 120 — The Solar System and the Universe

1) false — The Sun is a star.
2) comet (smallest), planet, star, galaxy (largest)

Page 121 — Asteroids and Comets

1) Mars and Jupiter
2) dust and ice

Page 122 — NEOs and the Moon

1) Asteroids or comets that are on a possible collision course with Earth/that could hit Earth.
2) The distance light travels in one year.

Page 123 — Understanding the Universe

1) unmanned
2) At the start, everything in the Universe was squashed into a tiny space. Then it exploded (in a big bang). Then it started expanding (spreading out) and hasn't stopped yet.

Page 124 — The Life Cycle of Stars

1) supernova
2) white dwarf

Page 125 — Galileo and Copernicus

1) the Earth
2) telescope
3) Galileo saw moons orbiting Jupiter. This showed not everything orbits the Earth.

Index

Index